MEMOIRS OF A SPECIAL CASE

By the same Author
(under the name of Jocelyn Davey)
★
THE UNDOUBTED DEED
THE NAKED VILLANY
A TOUCH OF STAGEFRIGHT

MEMOIRS OF
A SPECIAL CASE

Chaim Raphael

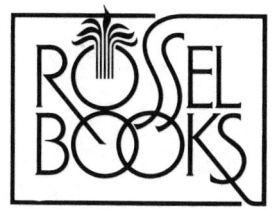

CHAPPAQUA, NEW YORK

COPYRIGHT 1947, 1950, 1953, © 1957, 1960, 1962
BY CHAIM RAPHAEL

ALL RIGHTS RESERVED. NO PART OF THIS BOOK MAY BE REPRODUCED IN ANY FORM WITHOUT PERMISSION IN WRITING FROM THE PUBLISHER, EXCEPT BY A REVIEWER WHO MAY QUOTE BRIEF PASSAGES IN A REVIEW TO BE PRINTED IN A MAGAZINE OR NEWSPAPER.

LIBRARY OF CONGRESS CATALOG CARD NO. 62-9548

REVISED EDITION, 1985

Several pieces from this book first appeared
in the *Atlantic Monthly* and *Commentary*.

International Standard Book Numbers:
ISBN 0-940646-16-1 (Cloth Edition)
ISBN 0-940646-17-X (Paperback Edition)

85 86 87 88 89   6 5 4 3 2

PRINTED IN THE UNITED STATES OF AMERICA

For
Diana, Adam and Jackie

'We are all special cases. We all want to appeal against something. Each of us insists at all costs that he is innocent, even if he has to accuse the whole human race and heaven itself.'

ALBERT CAMUS: *The Fall*

CONTENTS

Overture in New York	page 9
I	
Vic and Tubby	15
Malcah and Sedgewick	32
Jonas, My Old Friend	49
The Words and the Music	69
II	
Jerusalem	85
III	
The Special Case	183
And the Crisping Pins	201

OVERTURE IN NEW YORK

IT seemed very satisfying at the time to be a Jew in New York. Pat, who lived there and was a picture of the all-American dreamgirl with her wide-open eyes and a mixed assortment of Jewish and non-Jewish stepfathers and stepmothers, had said it to me one day in her own way as she stretched out her glass for a second martini: 'Everyone looks Jewish when you're in love.' It was a remark that could only be made in New York and that neatly divided an audience into two groups: those who thought it very funny *and true*, and those who found it peculiar and more than a little gauche. If one laughed at it in New York, one promptly tried to envisage who had first said it. Once it might have been S. J. Perelman; now, maybe Woody Allen. But no one really creates these great remarks: they simply float up by themselves from the New York scene.

There was a sense of great assurance in this kind of world. The fundamentals of life were predictable—such as that there would be a shortage of taxis on the streets on Yom Kippur. To be a Jew in New York meant that one was part of life's most responsive audience, laughing one's head off—when one was not bursting into tears, of course.

Behind the laughter there was always an enticing question: would New York reveal something new about the Jews? Things could happen elsewhere, but in New York, surely, it had all been finally added up. The world had never really had a chance to know what would happen if you took all that energy and curiosity and turned things upside down, so that the eternal minority was at last given its head. What happened was that the eternal minority grew to three million, developed fantastic wealth and strength, sent its force eddying out in waves of schmaltz and high purpose over the whole world—and remained the eternal minority.

So one had seen the whole thing in operation on yet another

stage—and *what* a stage. The old cast would of course give way to new performers—from Arthur Miller to Philip Roth, from Ben Shahn to Mark Rothko, from David Dubinsky to Mayor Edward Koch, from Milton Berle to Barbra Streisand—but it was still the same play, leaving the same question mark in the air. Perhaps the world had not waited long enough for a new meaning to be defined. Three thousand years of Jewish experience was too short a time. The Psalmist certainly seemed to think so. 'A thousand years in Thy sight is as yesterday when it is past and as a watch in the night.'

That was one way out: quote the Psalms—the perfect script for Madison Avenue, as good as Shakespeare for catchphrases that would really sell. And for the quiet moments when one might be at home taking in *Yentl* on one's $10,000 stereo video, looking out from one's fortieth storey penthouse across the Park with its miraculous backdrop of twinkling lights, one could find many a pearl of wisdom in the Psalms to satisfy the mind. *Oh Lord, how great are Thy works!* Surely New York was what the Psalmist had in mind. *The righteous shall flourish like the palm tree . . . they shall be fat and flourishing*, ready-made clients for Barney's, the shop on 17th Street which specializes in clothes for fat and flourishing men, and with free parking for customers.

God may by now have made up His mind about the Jews, or He may still be waiting. He has had a better chance than the rest of us to see it all in perspective. Those of us who are only here today and gone tomorrow have had to take the whole thing on the run almost. Even in a locale as monolithic as New York it was hard to pinpoint some consistently Jewish culture and way of life. The Jews may have inherited a culture of their own, but it seems to define itself best in the background of somebody else's. Even in Israel, what they have done is not to reproduce the culture of Abraham, Isaac and Jacob but the quintessence of nineteenth century liberalism—patriotism with its limitless power for sacrifice and self-satisfaction, a blind faith in science and music, parliamentary democracy at its most fissiparous, the Europe that the Jews were excluded from and

OVERTURE IN NEW YORK

have had to recreate for themselves. So Israel today is one of the few places where a newspaper still carries a long daily *feuilleton* in the old style, and a man who disagrees with another man's opinion will fight to the death for his right to outshout him. And if it be argued that the Israelis are in fact on their way to something entirely new as twentieth century Hebrews, this is *ipso facto* different from the datum of the *Galuth*, where the essential condition is that it must have gone on for two thousand years. Only in New York is there a new gloss to the story in this sense, which is, of course, what makes the place so absorbing.

All this may seem a far cry from the stories that are set out in this book and that hark back to my early years in England and Europe before I settled down to a long period of work in New York; but it is relevant for me because in letting my mind drift back to earlier times, it was precisely to recover from the exuberance of New York and set my feet firmly on the ground in the safe exactitude of small-scale existence—small countries, a small town, a small Jewish community, a few odd individuals exchanging a *Sholom Aleichem* or two while the non-Jewish world caught us up in its fate or passed by regardless. In New York seven years ago it was 'Stop the world, I want to get off,' and everybody knew what one meant. But on the Tyneside near Hadrian's Wall, or in the Cathedral Close at Lydford, or in Florence, or Cordova or pre-Israel Jerusalem, the world was never spinning fast enough to need stopping; one got on or off without difficulty, and one could even sit there quietly for a time. Remembering that quiet mood, it would be easier to set things apart, to hear the words as well as the music. That, anyhow, was what I felt when I went back to England after a dizzy spell of fifteen years in New York. Before I could catch up with New York I had to catch up with myself.

But the self is an elusive creature. At first, memories came back simply and factually, and I found it easy to put them down that way. But once I had unlocked the door, much more came through than I had bargained for, especially when I came to deal with my sojourn in prewar Jerusalem. Here the canvas was too big for me to be at the centre in purely realistic terms. As I wrote of Jerusalem in the days long before the State of Israel emerged, memories and dreams of many people and many things shook themselves free of time and place. I let it all flow, for if something impelled me to write this way in fact and fantasy, this too was part of the self I had been looking for.

I

VIC AND TUBBY

WITHIN a week of getting back to England I ran into Vic at the Dorchester. I had hardly seen him since our schooldays, but he had now become a famous name because of his fantastic take-over bids. One day he was buying up the Ritz and the next day all the breweries. But just that week, his name had been in the papers because of something unexpected from this kind of tycoon. He had appeared at a sale at Sotheby's, outbid some Americans for a unique collection of Donne manuscripts, and presented them to the British Museum. To the world at large this seemed like a bit of showmanship—a good piece of public relations to turn people's minds away from some of his more outrageous deals. But there was quite a different echo in it for me, knowing as I did that Donne was no stranger to this deliberately uncouth businessman. The real bit of public relations was to fool the British public with his pose of ruthless indifference to the niceties of life, so that he would be free, without anyone bothering him, to do the things that had value for him.

He had been this way at school. It was obvious that he would never change. Half the take-over bids that he started—especially the really startling ones, such as when he tried to buy the Athenaeum itself—never came off, and I always thought, remembering the schoolboy, that this too was part of the game. The public had their eyes fixed on the relatively conservative activities of Cotton and Clore. Well, Vic would show them, and if they didn't like it, to hell with them. The odd thing was that they *did* like it—or were at least fascinated by it, just as old Rabbi Taub, in whose house we had lived as schoolboys, had both feared and respected him.

I was out that evening with Arthur, another of our schoolboy gang. Arthur, who now worked for the British Council, had looked me up a few times when he had passed through New York on official work, and hearing that I was back had invited me to attend a British Council dinner at the Dorchester It was afterwards, when we had escaped into the lounge for a quiet drink and talk, that we bumped into Vic, who kept a flat there for business purposes. We greeted each other as if we had all been shipwrecked separately on the same deserted island—which in a way we had.

'My God!' I said to Vic. 'Let me look at you! You still look almost human. I wouldn't believe it from what I read in the papers.'

'Yeah,' Vic said, in his same old rough cockney voice. 'You'd think the blood was dripping from my fingers.'

'Nature red in tooth and Clore,' said Arthur, who has always had a gift—if that's what it is—for this kind of remark.

'Have you just made that up, brother?' Vic asked.

'No,' Arthur said. 'I've been saving it up for weeks. You've made my evening.'

'Wouldn't old Tubby have been delighted,' I said. 'About the manuscripts, I mean.'

'Goot vine in a bad wessel,' Arthur quoted, in Rabbi Taub's thick German accent. 'He always believed in you, Vic. You were his favourite.'

'He was a bastard,' Vic said, 'and he hated my guts. He would have told me where to buy the manuscripts cheaper, of course.'

'In the market, at eight in the morning, with the herrings, no doubt,' Arthur said: and then became Tubby again: 'Who is zis man Donne? Why not *Jewish* manuscripts?'

'It sent me way back,' I said musingly to Vic. 'Can you still quote Donne by the yard?'

'I wouldn't be surprised,' Vic said. '*O perplexed discomposition! O ridling distemper! O miserable condition of man!* No, I suppose I've forgotten the rest. Old age has crept up. All I can remember from school are those damned rhymes for learning Latin:

> *Common are to either sex*
> *Artifex and opifex.*'

'Useful names round here,' I murmured, looking at some delicate young men on the next table.

VIC AND TUBBY

Arthur broke in:

> '*Abstract nouns in -io call*
> *Feminina one and all.*
> *Masculine will only be*
> *Things that you can touch and see.*'

One of the young men looked up at this point, and we had some difficulty in not laughing. 'Bang on,' Vic said.

After all these years we were back at school again. What is it about English schools—especially boarding schools—that leaves such a mark on the English? Why should it only happen to the English?

Not that this was an ordinary school, or Rabbi Taub an ordinary schoolmaster. Nor were the ten of us who had lived in his home typical English schoolboys. Or if we were when we began, the atmosphere of that house must have done something to us.

★   ★   ★

Perhaps we learnt one lesson there: that there are no rules—for some people, anyhow. In the age-old pattern of English life outside at Fenner College, everything seemed to fall into ordered slots like a long row of suburban back-gardens; but for us there was a constant reminder in our daily routine that separate worlds can and do mingle for the greater fun of God and man. The Donne purchase was a natural part of the same Vic who had spoken always in the foulest cockney, argued Talmud with the most incisive of minds, and spouted Donne and Herbert both in fun and reverence.

'*Good wine in a bad vessel*' had been Rabbi Taub's description of him. Perhaps this was a translation of some Hebrew saying, for Tubby knew Hebrew if he knew nothing else. This was one of the revelations to all of us when we came to Fenner. All ten of us had grown up in orthodox Jewish backgrounds, and it had been a condition of our scholarships to Fenner that we could translate the Bible and some of the rabbinic writings. But we were all English born, and felt the pull of the secular life around us. Rabbi Taub, by contrast, had come late in life to this peaceful town in south-west England from a Jewish background in Lithuanian Russia, where to be a Jew was a complete experience. He had been born into that age of Jewish awakening in Eastern Europe when the revived Hebrew language became the key to a whole philosophy of nationalism. Yiddish was still his mother tongue, but Hebrew had been added—artificial in one sense but deeply satisfying in another. Many of his old friends had, of course, become the early Zionist pioneers. Tubby talked of them a lot—and that was just it: he *talked* about them. There was a flaw in him which had made him prefer a fleshpot here to an ideal lived out in the stony soil of Palestine. We recognized this as schoolboys, even though we were thrilled ourselves with the use of Hebrew as a living language.

What was so odd was to find this little enclave of modern Hebrew in the sleepy old cathedral town of Lydford. But then the whole existence of Fenner College was bizarre. An English Jew named Josiah Fenner, born and brought up in Lydford in the middle of the nineteenth century had made a sizeable fortune as a tea-merchant in India, and in his will had left all his money to found an academy in his native town to train young aspirants to the Jewish ministry. His family had fought the will desperately on the ground that it was self-evidently the act of a demented man, and about three-quarters of the bequest had been pleasantly dissipated in lawyers' fees during litigation that dragged on for about ten years. They had finally lost the case, however, and with the money that was left Fenner College had been opened in 1898 in a rambling old house close to Lydford's town park. In granting scholarships to would-be rabbis, the trustees of the college were instructed by the will to give preference to Jewish boys from Lydfordshire and India; but even this quaint combination did not apparently succeed in giving the institution much character until Rabbi Taub was appointed Principal.

By that time Lydfordshire and India had been drained dry of rabbinical candidates, and the ten of us—all about fourteen years old—who found ourselves its students soon after Tubby's appointment had come mostly from the north of England, attracted by the promise of a free secular education at the local grammar school, a thorough Jewish education under Rabbi Taub, and completely free board. It was a prize we had won by competitive examination; and we had all displayed latent talent even if our rabbinical tendencies were as yet undeveloped.

Tubby was supposed to see to that. His familiarity with Hebrew as a living tongue was surely a guarantee of his professional powers; and even if his immense girth and fruity voice did not strike a particularly religious note, there was an undeniable dignity in his snow-white hair and carefully trimmed Vandyke beard.

It didn't take us long to see that Tubby was no great rabbinic scholar, but we didn't hold this against him particularly. To us, his geniality—when he felt like it—and a certain zest for living were worth more than dry-as-dust scholarship; and we found it quite acceptable that in teaching us Talmud, or even the much easier Biblical commentary of Rashi, he should have to excuse himself from the schoolroom at frequent intervals to consult one of the many cribs which we had found one day in his study bookcase. Indeed we welcomed the interruptions since they enabled us to get on with our games of pontoon or poker, or—when it became the current craze—to compose contributions for each other's autograph albums.

No one could deny that when Tubby was well dressed and pomaded he looked like an aristocrat, even if, as we well knew, his true forte was the running of a profitable boarding-house. The fatal system adopted by the trustees was to give him a fixed and quite liberal allowance for each boy. Far from leaving catering problems to his wife, he took it all upon himself, with the greatest enthusiasm. Like a good innkeeper he was out early most days bargaining at the market for damaged apples, stale bread, rancid margarine, surplus barrels of herring—anything in fact that would satisfy our ravenous appetites without upsetting his idea of an appropriate budget. He would stand towering over us in the large kitchen-dining-room while Gladys, the maid-of-all-work, served it up; and when we were very young we preferred to eat it up, stale and bad as it often was, rather than provoke one of the rages which alternated continuously with his smiling good humour. Gradually we developed a system of dropping food that offended us into paper bags concealed under the table, making up for it by parcels from home or meals bought in cafés during the evening. Only later did we realize that he must have known all about our paper bags and café haunting and many other things. Perhaps we were open books to him: but did he ever guess that we may have ascribed equally strange things to him?

On the whole it is unlikely, for it was a long time since he had been a schoolboy, and he may not have understood that though food and study were always in the foreground at the college, they were never as important to us as our constant fumbling researches into sex. So proud was he of his place as the Principal that it would not have crossed his mind that we thought of him very rarely as Rabbi Taub and much more frequently as the podgy figure we sometimes saw sitting up in bed wearing long combinations, a faded green dressing-gown and a red night-cap, and being ministered to in some undefinable way by the sour, bony Gladys. The thought of an interesting relationship had first come to me when I was reciting one Sabbath in our little synagogue the scriptural reading from the Book of Kings: '*Now King David was old, stricken in years, and they covered him in garments, but he gat no heat. Wherefore his servants said unto him: Let there be sought for my lord the king a young virgin, and let her stand before the king and let her cherish him, and let her lie in his bosom that my lord the king may get heat.*' When I put the point to the boys afterwards, they were quite ready to concede its possibility. Mrs Taub, we agreed, was no longer in the picture. Gladys, on the other hand, Vic insisted, was no virgin. But we could concede, in theory, that she could probably warm up any man. It was true that none of us ever got near her, and only one of us, a rather gross creature called Bernard, ever indulged with her in our normal schoolboy improprieties. But Tubby, we began to notice, had a certain tenderness towards her, very different from his rudeness towards his wife and the rest of us. For all her boniness, Gladys had a certain cheap prettiness, and when she was dressed and scented to go out on her afternoon off, there was a distinctly feminine feeling in the air. Sometimes we would see her go by as we sat in the schoolroom with Tubby, going over a passage from the Talmud: *Two men pick up a garment. If one says: I found it, and the other says: I found it, they must divide it equally. If one says: It is all mine and the other says: It is half mine, then Rabbi Gamaliel says* . . . But it was all a little unreal, for as Gladys passed the open door she left the smell of her cheap powder in the air for an old man and ten sex-hungry rabbinical students.

* * *

The mystery was—and is—how anyone could expect young boys to study the Bible closely and not be obsessed by its sexual freedom, so remote in spirit from the Jewish—or Victorian—prudery of those very elders who forced the Bible on their young. For me it was not a question of having to look for the dirty passages. The whole Bible, and especially the Pentateuch, was our daily and detailed concern. We translated it all constantly, with rabbinical commentaries. We chanted the weekly portion in the synagogue. Perhaps there was extra fun in this for us, chanting the verses (which we well understood) to outsiders who were mostly ignorant of Hebrew even though they could read it. It was fairly natural for a schoolboy of fifteen, working his way in the age-old sing-song through the story of Joseph and Potiphar's wife, to linger with special devotion on the moment where she cries out to him: 'Sleep with me, sleep with me!'

The whole story of Joseph was as satisfying as the weekly movie. But what had a particular fascination for me was not so much the fully worked out stories as those strange interruptions which occur all over Genesis, where the story-teller harks back (sometimes in a more ancient Hebrew) to half-remembered myths and tales, a line or two from an archaic song, a character seen in a magic twilight. I remember how, in the middle of reading the story of Joseph, I was suddenly struck for the first time with the story of Judah and Tamar, and how I lay on my bed that night filling it out with endless imagination. It is one whole chapter, the thirty-eighth chapter of Genesis, inserted as a complete break into the story of Joseph. The previous chapter has ended in suspense—like the *Perils of Pauline*—with Joseph sold as a slave into Egypt; <u>and suddenly, forgetting Joseph, the writer tells us a story about his brother Judah, who had a full life, one might say, among non-Jews.</u> How close one feels to Judah. Subjected all his life, no doubt, to endless hectoring about Abraham, Isaac, and Jacob, he finds it too much—breaks away from his brothers, becomes the close friend of 'a certain Adullamite', and falls in with 'the daughter of a certain Canaanite', who bears him three sons. How simply it is all told in two opening sentences, and how gentle is our introduction to Tamar, the wife he finds for his first son. From the very beginning there seems to be some special relation between Judah and Tamar. <u>The first son dies: Tamar marries the second son, the unspeakable Onan, who prefers to spill his seed on the ground rather than give her a child.</u> He too dies, and she waits for the third son, Shelah, to be old enough to marry her. But something holds Judah back from agreeing to the marriage; and it is then— in despair, or perhaps in love—that she plays her trick on Judah, disguising herself as a prostitute and waiting by the roadside to catch him on his way to the sheep-shearing. Judah, quite unaware of who she is, feels drawn to her with a mysterious passion. She finds herself with child by him, and returns to her own village. <u>But the neighbours, seeing her pregnant and without a husband, denounce her—to her father-in-law Judah.</u> He has never seen the face of the woman he met by the roadside, and in anger at the disgrace to his family, orders her to be burnt. She is brought to him, names him as the father and proves it by the ring he gave her. Judah, struck with remorse, sees himself and Tamar in a clear light for the first time. He asks for her forgiveness. And the writer adds one sentence: 'he never slept with her again.'

Who were these remote people, my ancestors? As a schoolboy I thought of the patriarchs as wise old men with long beards like the Dutch Jews whom Rembrandt painted. Judah I saw as an Arab Sheikh. But in later years, when I first saw Hittite and Sumerian statuettes—the wild distortion of eyes and ears, the immense power given to a gargantuan nose, the enormous weight of head on a small base of curled-up legs—I began to feel in the magic exaggeration of the artist the real force of the archaic stories of Genesis. These were far-off magic men, very unlike Karl Marx and Lord Rothschild, and very unlike Rabbi Taub, getting up from the evening lesson to go down to the kitchen and make the cocoa, with Gladys at his side.

★ ★ ★

Every morning we went off to Lydford Grammar School, and at first there were no problems. We were scattered in different classes and were usually top of the class since we were, after all, scholarship boys, with Vic outstanding for his analytical mind, his fantastic memory and his colossal impertinence. But one day a new headmaster—Sedgewick—arrived, and began to wage with Tubby a startling, if subtle, battle for the salvation of our souls. Sedgewick, a Christian clergyman, product of Winchester and Oxford, grasped immediately the paradoxes of Fenner College. The cool grey learning of Winchester, the scrupulous humanism of the Greeks, the passion of Cimabue and Giotto were Sedgewick's weapons, and powerful they were. Oddly enough, when we climbed out at night, as we often did, to see if we could find some girls to flirt with in the park, it was Sedgewick's world that we took with us. Girls were scarce, and we would walk around talking—of books we had read, ideas that had come to us in school.

'Know what happened today?' Vic said one night when we were out walking. 'Beetles got sore as hell in physics and sent me off to the Head.'

'Why, what had you done?'

'Hadn't done a bloody thing—just had a bit of an argument.'

'Funny. Beetles is usually pretty easy.'
'Oh yes, he's all right, but I just got tired of him today. He's so bloody steady. Know what I mean? Just think of him, doing the same bloody experiments year after year—always ready with the same questions, the same little tricks to catch us, the same tame little jokes. Nothing surprising has ever happened to him: so instead of doing the question I started an argument with him about the nature of matter. God, he got sore. You know that squeaky high-pitched voice. I bet he's a castrate. "This isn't a philosophy class: we just try to content ourselves with a few humble experiments." Humble experiments. God, how I hate that crap. I said: "Look, brother. Do you think that Einstein and Minkowski would have got anywhere with that attitude to physics? They asked questions. They didn't do what they were told. . . ."'
'Crikey, what did he say?'
'Nearly exploded. Marched me off to the Head and left me there. The Head was pretty good. Know what he did? Kept me sitting there for about ten minutes while he pulled a book out of his shelf, read through it for a bit, wrote something on the fly-leaf and gave it to me. He said: "I gather from Mr Beeton that you want to develop your undoubted gifts for philosophical speculation. Read this and you will discover that courtesy is an integral element in argument." Know what the book was?'
'How would *I* know?'
'Plato's *Republic*. Just gave it to me as a present. And he'd written on the fly-leaf: *From Book IV*: "*To exact of young men a proper silence in presence of their elders.*" Bloody marvellous man, really.'
'Golly: is that all he did?'
'No, blast him. He's taken me off the team to debate with the Astonbury Girls' School next Wednesday. Something about: "I'm sure you wouldn't want to upset the girls with your methods of argument." And I was looking forward to it, damn him. Whole afternoon and evening off—and there's a bird there I picked out when they came here last month—a real

juicy bit. Do you think he knew? Wouldn't put it beyond him. . . .'

Sedgewick was on his way, and the odds were weighted heavily in his favour. But there were weapons in Tubby's armoury too, despite his own inability to use them. Night after night as we sat in the schoolroom ploughing our way through Bible and Talmud, we would feel a terrible boredom sinking in on us; but then the majesty of Isaiah—the marvellous cadences —would come breaking through; or one of us would start explaining a Talmudic point to the rest of the class, and would be seized with the sheer beauty of the argument.

It was usually Vic, and as he launched himself into the rabbi's dictum, he would grow enthusiastic in developing its ramifications. The rabbi, he might explain, has quoted the Biblical verse in question not for its direct meaning but because of some hidden association of letters within the verse, an anagram or similar form, which reminds him of a similar anagram in some other Biblical verse, where a law is enjoined which must not, of course, be taken literally but again interpreted by analogy with a traditional explanation of another prophetic saying, itself susceptible perhaps of three meanings, two of which are excluded because of some logical inconsistency, while the third is the focal point of this injunction and is proved to be valid, incidentally, because its converse would be untrue. Having established this first point, it becomes important to know if the rabbi could really have meant what he seems to have said, since in some other book of the Talmud he is quoted by another rabbi as saying something which might be interpreted as inconsistent with it. The simplest solution to this problem is to show that both statements are untrue, which relieves the rabbi of inconsistency and allows the view to be advanced of one of the earlier 'founding father' rabbis who, according to the rules of the game, can never be accused of inaccuracy. Their 'tradents', however, can; and it is the easiest thing in the world to throw doubt on the reliability of this or that reporter of an earlier rabbi's saying. At this point an anecdote is introduced, not for its own sake but for a sting in the tail—perhaps to show that the man reporting the saying never even knew the rabbi he is claiming to report. . . .

Tubby would sit back listening to Vic explain all this and nodding with happy approval. Perhaps he would be so pleased that he would magnanimously end the lesson. Earlier in the day he might have been raging at Vic for some act of flat disobedience. When he raged he would go purple, shouting: 'Zat blackguard! He sinks he is master here! I will show him ze door!' But now, as we sat drinking our cocoa and chattering happily, he would look at Vic with affection and a certain wonder, and murmur: 'Goot vine in a bad wessel! Goot vine in a bad wessel!'

★ ★ ★

Tubby's difficulty with the English language was not merely comic. It had a deeper significance. English was for Tubby the symbol of an attempt on his part to meet the western world on equal terms, and his failure at this was absolute. It was laid down by the trustees, for example, that in our first year at Fenner we should study not merely the Bible and Talmud but also later Jewish history, in the same way as we studied English history at school. Tubby, unfortunately, knew as much schematic Jewish history as the average Englishman knows about Alfred the Great. To meet the need he got hold of some textbooks from America written in a style like this: '*On a beautiful spring day in the year 1145, the streets of Cordova, Spain, were filled with a happy throng gathered to celebrate the appointment of a new Caliph. Standing quietly under a moorish arch was a serious-looking young boy called Moses, holding his father Maimon by the hand. Little did the passers-by realize that this small boy with the deep questioning eyes was destined to become the greatest scholar Jewry had ever known, the philosopher and scientist Maimonides.*'

We would be given a half hour for preparation and then a test:

'Wiz what were ze streets from Cordova filled?'

Answer: 'With a happy throng.'

VIC AND TUBBY

'What did ze passers-by not realize?'

Answer: 'That Moses would become Maimonides.'

But hilarious as he was in English, Tubby could approach us in one way that transformed our relationship—when he delivered a sermon in Yiddish. In Yiddish he threw off the mask and spoke to us not as the Principal of Fenner College but as a Jew from Russia, his heart full of the anguish of his people. His Yiddish was not the corrupt jargon that we had heard so frequently in our childhood. It had an elevation and expressiveness that made it sound to us like Elizabethan English; and when he spoke it in synagogue, lapsing into the unearthly sing-song of the true *maggid*, it affected his whole being, linking him with that inchoate but living background in which he had once been a real person.

On most Saturdays his sermon to us in our little synagogue was delivered in his usual pidgin English, and we had to pass the time as best we could by discreetly playing word games, or making up parodies on familiar poems. But on Holydays, when our synagogue was crowded with visitors, he would somehow recognize an overpowering need to speak in his mother tongue, and it would transform him.

I have never forgotten the mood of his Yiddish sermon on one Day of Atonement, at the closing service—*Neila*. Dusk had set in, and with the approaching end of the twenty-four-hour fast there was a tenseness unfamiliar in our gatherings. Tubby stood at the reading desk facing us, his great bulk wrapped in a white *kittel*, his white hair and beard glistening in the light of the one lamp that burned perpetually.

'When the *Neila* moment comes,' he said, 'the day grows dark; for when the time of *Neila* comes it grows dark in our hearts.'

And thence he went on to talk of this unique day as itself a cycle of life and death for each one of us. We understand our own emptiness only when the light of life fades irrevocably away. Each prayer and each *mea culpa* of Yom Kippur becomes clear to us only when the obscurity of daylight vanishes, leaving us face to face with the clarity of darkness. He told us how, within an hour, we would approach the climax of the *Neila* service, and repeat with the holy intensity of dying men the *Shema Yisrael*. A dying man repeats the *Shema*, he said, not as a prayer but as the most passionate expression of faith in himself as part of Israel. As he dies, he shares in the martyrdom of Israel when rabbis, wrapped in the sacred scroll and thrown into the flames, perished with the *Shema* triumphant on their lips and with the holy letters of the scroll flying miraculously out of the fire. '*Otiot porchot!*' he cried, bursting into Hebrew, the tears streaming down his cheeks—'the letters flew out!'

* * *

When the Fast was over and we had supposedly retired for the night, Vic, Arthur, and I climbed out for a stroll in the park. It was a lovely autumn evening, and in the distance we could see across the park the delicate spire of Lydford Cathedral.

'Old Tubby can certainly talk in Yiddish,' Vic said. 'He hit me right in the solar plexus.'

'It's funny though,' I said, 'that the only way he can get us is to talk about death.'

'Christ!' said Vic. 'I don't mean what he said. It's the bloody marvellous way he said it.'

'I don't know,' I said. 'I kept thinking while he was speaking how similar it was to that piece from John Donne that you wrote in my album.'

'Some difference,' said Vic. 'Old Tubby was asking us to torment ourselves with the thought of death, and old Donne was saying: grow up.'

And as we stood leaning on a stone balustrade overlooking the park lake, Vic began to recite the piece from Donne's own funeral sermon that he had learnt by heart:

'Is this the honour which man hath by being a little world? Is he a world to himself only, therefore, that he hath enough in himself not only to destroy and execute himself, but to presage that execution upon himself, to assist the sickness, to make the sickness more irremediable by sad apprehension, and as if he would make a fire the more vehement by sprinkling water upon the coals, so to wrap a hot fever in cold melancholy, lest the fever should not destroy fast enough without this contribution, nor perfect the work (which is destruction) except we joined an artificial sickliness of our own melancholy to our natural, our unnatural fever. O perplexed discomposition! O ridling distemper! O miserable condition of man!'

We were silent for a little while.

'Isn't miserable a wonderful word?' said Arthur. 'Almost as wonderful as misericordia. "O miserable condition of mankind, where one half lacks meat and the other stomach!"'

'Donne was always thinking about death in one way or another,' I said:

> *But since that I*
> *Must die at last, 'tis best*
> *To use myself in jest*
> *Thus by feigned deaths to die.'*

'That, brother,' said Vic, 'was when he was parting from one of his birds. And talking of birds, what do my eyes see?'

Sure enough, three girls were coming in our direction. We walked along towards them, exchanged greetings, and spent quite a time bantering and fooling before we went home and climbed in.

★ ★ ★

It was easy enough to joke about sex—we seemed to spend half our time at it; but the real question was how to make it real. We shared many confidences but not all, and it was Vic that was the real mystery to me. He was a year older than me, but it wasn't this. He seemed to have some ease that I lacked. Something obscure in me always held me back. When we slipped out sometimes to go to a dance at the Parish Hall, Vic would take the prettiest girl and dance with her all evening, while I would stand hesitantly near the door waiting for whoever came my way. At fourteen he looked eighteen: at sixteen he was like a fully-grown man; and we took it for granted that while we bantered about sex, he spoke from experience.

We shared a bedroom, and one summer night, after a long discussion through most of the evening on Keats and Shelley, whom we were reading at school, we lay quietly in our beds smoking a last cigarette and rolling over on our tongues the luscious stanzas of *La Belle Dame Sans Merci*. At the back of my mind for several days was an incident which I had half overseen and which had both aroused and frustrated me.

Tubby had a close friend, a doctor from Germany, who had been staying at the College for a little while with his wife, very much younger than himself—a big comfortable-looking woman called Elsa. We saw a lot of them; they were treated like members of the family. They had a room on the second floor, and one day, while alone outside the playroom (which was on the floor below) I heard Elsa call to Vic as he was passing her door. I saw her open the door wider and stand there, her nightgown covered only by a dressing-gown, and that hanging loosely enough to give me a sudden jolt and send my blood pounding.

'Are you off to school?' she asked.

Vic looked at her. 'You ought to pull yourself together,' he said. 'You're a big girl now,' and he touched her half-revealed breast familiarly.

'You cheeky thing,' she said. 'Come in a minute. I want to ask you something.'

Vic went in and closed the door, and I ran downstairs and out into the garden, burning and miserable. When I thought of it later, the story of Judah and Tamar came into my mind. I saw Tamar, her face covered by a veil, waiting for Judah outside her tent on the dusty road to Timnath, so full of desire and yet so fearful of the harlot's trick through which she sought to soften the pain of widowhood.

Now, as Vic and I lay smoking, I said to him: 'What do you think of Elsa?'

'She's just a whore,' he said slowly. 'What makes you ask?'

'I saw her ask you into her room the other day,' I said. 'I wondered what happened.'

'Nothing happened,' he said. 'She's a bitch, and I hate bitches.'

'Didn't she want something?'

'Look, brother,' said Vic. 'You know what she wanted as well as I do, but I don't like the girl to ask me. I like to do the asking. I don't know what difference it really makes. It all comes to the same in the end, but I just don't like it. When I got inside her room I just spat in her eye and left it at that. I tell you another funny thing. I felt sorry for old Tubby. He would have felt pretty low if he'd found out. . . .'

'Funny thing,' he added after a pause. 'It's just occurred to me. I suppose that's what stopped Joseph. He was sorry for old Potiphar. . . . They're all a lot of bitches. . . .'

Bitches or not, I lay awake wondering how Vic and Joseph could act that way. It seemed to me that if I were in their shoes . . . but that was just it. I wasn't in their shoes. No woman would pick me out for her favours. . . .

Why was I so worried about it? Why couldn't I be as easygoing as the others? I was different in some way. Sometimes the difference was satisfying. In the last few weeks Sedgewick had picked me out for special attention. He was encouraging me to work for a scholarship to Oxford. That part was fine. But that was at school. When school was over one wanted so many other things that lay beyond one's reach. Long long ago—at home in the north of England—there had been no such struggle. My father would give me a Hebrew lesson in the evening, and then a penny for learning so quickly what he taught me. My mother would be waiting with supper, warm and tasty. But my father was now away in Canada, and my mother had a struggle to keep our little home going. Did the tears come into my eyes when I thought of this, or did I look across the room at Vic, snoring heavily, arrogant, independent, the world waiting all unknowing at his feet for a good hearty kick. I can't remember.

MALCAH AND SEDGEWICK

IT was some time before I found myself near enough to Lydford to drive over and wander through the quiet streets. Sedgewick had left the Grammar School, not long after I had left myself, to become Dean of the Cathedral, and his very occasional letters to me had been written from his book-lined study overlooking the Cathedral Close.

It was his last letter that I was thinking of now as I walked around the Close. He had written to me in New York in 1948 at the height of the struggle in Palestine between the Jews and the British. Two years later he had died.

On the very same day on which his letter had arrived, I had had a letter from Palestine giving me the news that a young woman I knew there—Malcah—had been shot by the British, as one of a group of terrorists rounding up some stray British soldiers as hostages. Perhaps it was not so strange to have received news of Malcah and Sedgewick on the same day. Our world narrows around us as we grow older. Their paths had almost crossed in life, and now at last in these two letters they had come together.

Sedgewick had written to me across the waste of years impelled by a desire to express his deep misery at the fight between the British and the Jews.

'The more violent and criminal the terrorists become,' he wrote, 'the more sure I am that at some point the British have taken the wrong road morally in Palestine. I am horror-stricken at the things your people are doing there, and I support everything we are doing to repress the terrorists. Yet I know in my heart—I must as a Christian—that a story of Jewish bloodshed and suffering in Palestine can never be some accident of history. It is too close to another story of suffering that has eternal meaning for me. I have tried to read the meaning of the Jewish story so often, but I can never know if I have the answer. . . .'

MALCAH AND SEDGEWICK

Such, in effect, was Malcah's obituary. She would not have liked it.

I had put the letter in my pocket, carrying it and the thought of Malcah with me as I walked in the bleak wintry air along Riverside Drive. In the stolid, well-clad figures around me, so many coming from Malcah's own past, I had felt a quality of soft comfort hard to relate to her, and harder still to link in spirit to the rich asceticism of the Cathedral Close. Perhaps one day it would all fall into pattern, just as today it was no longer difficult to explain Malcah to Sedgewick. In Florence, all those years ago it had been unthinkable.

I was eighteen, and working hard at school for the scholarship that would take me to Oxford, when Sedgewick had sprung his surprise. Life had begun to take on a new shape. Vic had left the 'college', contemptuous of the need for any more book-studying and ready to plunge into business. The rest of us had gone on in many ways as before; English schoolboys by day, but at night and at each week-end as shut off from England as medieval Talmud students. Hour after hour we still sat around a large table under the watchful eye of Rabbi Taub, puzzling our way, with the help of the commentaries, through the old rabbinic writings. But even Tubby looked with veneration on the word *Oxford*, and during this special period I had been relieved of Talmud and almost all other Hebrew studies in order to bend my energies towards the coming examination.

Sedgewick had become my guardian angel through all this, setting me subjects himself for essays which I read to him long after the other boys had left school, or passing me on to his wife for coaching in economics and history. Tubby liked this too, that the Headmaster—and especially one who was a clergyman of the Church of England—should show such favour to one of the 'college boys'. But Tubby did not understand that I loved Sedgewick not so much for the lessons he gave me as for the bubbling jollity that he brought to everything, the clean-shaven parson's face dissolving into the schoolboy's grin, his eyes twinkling with fun when they were not filmed with a far-off mystic look.

33

MEMOIRS OF A SPECIAL CASE

Term was nearly over, and four weeks of Christmas vacation lay ahead, in which I was to keep my mind on nothing but my books. On this raw December morning, Sedgewick had just come out of prayers, and seeing me standing in the quad threw his arm around my shoulder, steered me towards his study, and, as if the whole thing were quite spontaneous and unimportant, said:

'Mrs Sedgewick and I are going to Florence next Monday for three weeks. We go every year for the Christmas holidays. Would you like to come with us as our guest? It would be such fun to be there together.'

Nothing since in my whole life has given me, or ever could give me, such a sense of ecstatic and bounding wonder. Sedgewick's words—quiet, almost careless—were like the opening statement of a fugue, a remark simple in itself that is destined to release a mighty flood of action and counteraction, a tumbling cataract of sound and beauty, before it achieves again the triumphant simplicity of completion. For me, all that went on in the next six days had just this feeling of crescendous excitement. For three days, Tubby and my school friends buzzed around me, echoing my own happiness and wonder. It was with a sense of almost uninterrupted movement from that first word with Sedgewick that we finished at school, swung into the train at London, buffeted our way across the Channel, touched a starry Paris at night with a kiss of welcome and farewell, and were heady with the frosty air of the Vosges and Alps. Breakfast at Basel, Domodossola behind us, and we were sweeping down to Bologna and Florence. *Rallentando*—and then the final triumphant single note ending the fugue, in a sound that died away in silence. I stood at the window of my own room in our hotel on the Lungarno, overlooking the Ponte Vecchio. I stood there for a long time alone. It was the first time that I had ever felt with any personal intimacy the brooding silence of the centuries.

It was, of course, this silence that Sedgewick wanted me to hear above the clatter of the schoolroom and the chatter of the textbooks. We were to go on as before with our meticulous studies, with names and authorities and dates, but only as background to a calm and unhurried intimacy with the golden mood of that ageless city. We were still the Headmaster and the favoured pupil, yet there was something deeper in our relationship that even now I cannot define. I sensed, of course, behind the exquisite generosity of Sedgewick's act, his own happiness at being able to re-live, through me, his own first rapture; but I felt also that since we were Christian and Jew in no passive sense, our relationship was enriched by some interplay of these two experiences. It was an equal interchange; there was never argument or pressure. But was there not, in Sedgewick's sweetness and understanding, a gentle assertion of the all-embracing truth and charity of Christianity?

It opened a strange world, buried as I had been in my books, to see reflected in Sedgewick's face the joyful holiness of a Fra Angelico, or to share with him, as we crossed the Piazza del Duomo, the unearthly lightness of the Campanile. A feeling of this kind was new to me, and I surrendered myself to it almost completely. Almost, but not wholly. Sometimes, as I trod the galleries or wandered through an incense-laden church to search out some primitive frescoes, I found myself full of my own thoughts, herding much of my new experience into a box labelled <u>Life among the Goyim</u>. How ruefully I look back now to those days, wondering who was fooling whom, and wondering too, as I think of his letter and Malcah, whether I shall ever find out why we make it all so difficult for ourselves.

★ ★ ★

We sat—Sedgewick, his wife, and I—at our table in the corner of the dining-room at the Hotel Grande Bretagne in Florence, the Headmaster, with the wine list before him, beaming with beneficence at all the world as he prepared to announce his decision. He squinted at me over the top of his glasses, and pressed the tips of his fingers together in prayerful cheerfulness.

'A bottle of Orvieto I think, eh? We must begin to break

away from Chianti. I wager that Horace drank Orvieto, and Horace knew. *Nunc est bibendum* . . .'

'*Nunc pede libero pulsanda tellus,*' I concluded dutifully.

'Ah, yes.' His happiness was complete. 'What a day it has been. That glorious Lippi.' He was quiet for a moment. 'And tomorrow,' he said, turning to me, 'Mrs Sedgewick and I will go to Santa Croce again, eh, while you go to synagogue?'

He lingered lovingly over the name *Santa Croce*, and I sensed the moment of holiness that would seize them the next day as they walked by the crude black and white marble of the façade into the cold majesty of the interior. We had been there once together some days earlier. Now once again they would breathe in the spirit of those high-sprung arches, and move slowly across the softly red floor towards the Giotto frescoes in the Bardi Chapel. Later they would come back into the Piazza—eyes averted from the horrid Dante statue (modern)—to go into the Cloisters, the first, by Arnolfo, to be smiled at tolerantly as a little too ornate, the second—the Brunelleschi—to be greeted with a gentle sigh of welcome.

In the beatific silence, the waiter returned and the Headmaster poured out the Orvieto. It seemed like a libation, a sort of *kiddush*.

It was Friday night, of course, that made it into *kiddush*. Back at the college old Tubby would be making a libation too, of rosy Carmel wine, and without benefit of Horace. At supper they would look at my empty place, and wonder, as I still did, how it had happened to me. I had had a letter that day from Arthur, pleasantly evocative of the college and our schoolboy pomposities:

'We all went to the Goldberg wedding on Tuesday night,' Arthur wrote. 'There was dancing and any amount of champagne until 2 a.m. Tubby generously turned a blind eye. It was all rather vulgar and most enjoyable.

'Life goes on here, as you see, the same as ever, and we can't yet determine whether it's we who are real and your journey that is fantasy, or vice versa. I strongly suspect that it is the latter, and that you have entered the real world, leaving us still buried in the cobwebs of make-believe. Sometimes I find myself asking the same kind of question at school, when we, gathered from the four corners of Minsk, Pinsk, and Brest Litovsk, bend our minds—and not unsuccessfully—to the study of our great English heritage, breathing the air that Shakespeare breathed, and calling for courage on the spirit of Drake, Nelson, and Kitchener. But "who fished the Midrash up? What porridge had Ibn Ezra?"'

I wrote a short note back to Arthur that night, saying cryptically that I would have much to tell him when I got back. He should remind me, I said, to tell him about a dark lady of the sonnets who had crossed my path.

'As for my being here,' I wrote, 'I think your first hypothesis is more correct. No one could call this a real world. Try and visualize Dante sitting in the Piazza, as he did, watching Giotto build the Duomo. Or think of this. When the city fathers were undecided where to put Michelangelo's *David*, they set up a committee to consider the question, the members being— now hold your breath—Perugino, Lorenzo di Credi, Filippino Lippi, Andrea della Robbia, Botticelli, and Leonardo da Vinci. Does this seem real?'

★ ★ ★

A daily ration of letter-writing was part of our usual routine before we settled down after dinner, in our corner of the hotel's vast drawing-room, to evening reading. Mrs Sedgewick usually began her evening with that part of Baedeker—in German— which covered the next day's activity, followed by a mighty Government blue book that she was working through—*The Report of the Balfour Committee on Industry and Trade*. The Headmaster was re-reading Vasari—in Italian—gurgling with pleasure every so often, until, at a later stage of the evening, he would lay it aside and pick up a grey-covered book of devotion that he had brought with him. *My* book, gently but firmly assigned to me from the first evening, was Creighton's *History of the Papacy*; but as I settled down to it each night, pursuing in particular the remarkable history of Aeneas Sylvius Piccolomini,

I would try desperately to put off the effort of absorption, reluctant to leave the bright, exciting world around me.

In the drawing-room itself, odd groups of diners would still be chattering away over their liqueurs, mostly English it seemed, but occasionally exotic-looking Latins, the women highly made-up, the men full of exaggerated mannerisms of politeness, helping the women fulsomely into their cloaks, or even kissing their hands in greeting. From outside, I would hear the pulse-quickening music of a foreign city—cafés, bars, the Opera—a world of freedom and life.

I would open my book slowly, lingering over the elaborate title-page: *A History of the Papacy From the Time of the Great Schism to the Sack of Rome, In Six Volumes, By Mandell Creighton, Bishop of London, 1901*; or I would turn in pleasant reverie to the end pages where, according to the formula of a more leisurely age, the publishers had printed their full current catalogue. It was so easy to let one's mind wander among those charmingly encrusted titles—books in the Badminton Library of Sports, edited by His Grace the Duke of Beaufort, books in the Fur, Feather, and Fin Series, books of travel and adventure in the Colonies—*With Rifle and Hound in Ceylon*—books of military adventure—*London to Ladysmith via Pretoria*, by Winston S. Churchill. . . .

But I would feel Sedgewick's eye on me, and would plunge again into the meteoric career of my hero Aeneas Sylvius, the man-about-town who became Pope Pius III. Even here, my mind would wander, awakening to the new world around me. What did it take to produce a distinguished churchman, I asked myself, thinking of Sedgewick's saintly poise? Aeneas Sylvius, as I knew from Creighton, had had many a carefree adventure before he entered the Church. 'His private life was profligate enough,' I read, 'but in 1446 he resolved to live more cleanly: "to abandon," as he said, "Venus for Bacchus." ' How had this charming world, so full of zest and the essence of living, been shrouded in the cold wrappers of the Reformation? What had impelled Creighton, a Protestant, to devote himself to it, writing long into the night in his no-doubt bleak and draughty vicarage in Northumberland? And Sedgewick, coming back every year from his grubby schoolboys to the idyllic infants of Della Robbia and the earthy peasants of Masaccio's *Holy Family*, did he too feel, as I did, that the fountain of life had ceased to flow freely in our cold, industrious climate, when man no longer made man in God's image?

I was beginning slowly and unsurely to find my way around the period, but there was a secret of taste, some canon of purity, which I realized I had not yet discovered. Andrea del Sarto was one test. One had to find his work 'too slick', 'insincere', though it looked beautiful enough to me. Cellini was another. One might read the *Memoirs* for fun, admire the *Perseus* as tremendously able, but essentially one had to recognize Cellini as a second-rater, a boaster, and a scallywag. But what if his sense of excitement seemed more liberating to a schoolboy than Savonarola's dour prophecies of doom? Well, one had to grow out of it. Cellini's adventures were not for the likes of us. Anyhow he was 'late'. He wasn't born until 1500.

This date was all-important. Everything really creative, I learned, had come to full flower by 1492, the year of Lorenzo's death. Nothing had the same interest after. The mighty years were 1300 to 1500, roughly speaking, and sometimes I tried to bring myself closer by asking what my own ancestors were doing in that choice age. It was not difficult to find a formula that said everything. The Jews were expelled from England in 1290 and expelled from Spain in 1492. That just about covered the period nicely.

'What kind of a man was Creighton?' I had asked Sedgewick. 'How did he come to devote himself to this period?'

'Oh, a great man,' said Sedgewick. 'He was trying desperately all his life to find out how Rome came to lose half of Europe, whether it had been inevitable, and what did it mean. Later, when he was Bishop of London, it became a very real problem, for he was the centre of a tremendous struggle on incense and ritual. He had to take a very firm line. It needed courage . . . and knowledge . . . and he had both.'

★   ★   ★

But my mind was not on Creighton that night. If anything, I was more in Cellini's world. The night before I had excused myself early, at about 9.30, but instead of going to my room had slipped out of the hotel, driven by an urge to savour Florence for myself. Where did the people go who left the hotel in the evening with such glittering cheerfulness? Perhaps in a café, or at the Opera, or in some dark glance thrown at me from a balcony or in a narrow cobbled street, I would meet the Florence of Benvenuto. The sap of life was bursting in me as I wandered happily through the crowd in the Via Tornabuoni.

I knew almost no Italian, but the gaiety of the chatter around me caught me up and I was suddenly enchanted to hear a joyful sound of music coming from nearby. Music in Italy! This is what I had been missing, and I moved towards it. As I approached I realized that it was even more heart-warming than I had thought. A troupe of five Austrian youths, dressed in traditional Tyrolean costume, were standing in a corner of the Piazza playing student songs on an odd variety of instruments—a violin, an accordion, a guitar, and a clarinet—while the fifth, a handsome fair-haired lad carrying a placard stating simply in Italian: 'We are walking to Rome', took around a collecting box. Occasionally two or three of the boys would sing out a chorus in simple harmony. Against this festive sound, the street-cars and carriages clattered by busily. Adding their own joy, the street lamps and café windows threw a dancing light on the soaring towers. The faces around were smiling and carefree.

As I stood there in the crowd, I became aware that a girl near me had begun to sing one of the songs with the students, a rollicking song that she was singing softly and nostalgically. She had a low, warm voice. I caught the words:

> '*Studio auf einer Reis*'
> *Juch heidi, juch heida.*
> *Ganz famos zu leben weiss,*
> *Juch heidi, juch heida.*'

When she saw me looking at her, she broke into a smile, the

MALCAH AND SEDGEWICK

deep smile that comes only when one is singing happily. She was young, dark, and shabbily dressed, but her face had the warmth that one finds in Italian women. The song had ended, and I smiled back, moved towards her, and braced myself for the effort to be gallant and devil-may-care in a language I hardly understood. My heart pumped away rapidly as I muttered something about her nice voice. I saw that she was looking at me searchingly, and when she spoke I knew what she thought she had seen in me.

'*Sind Sie Jude?*' she said.

Shades of Benvenuto Cellini! So much for the young Englishman abroad, the spiritual heir of Laurence Sterne and Lord Byron. *Sind Sie Jude!*

My German was rough but adequate.

'Yes, I am a Jew.'

This time the smile was one of real welcome.

'Where do you come from? I know you are not an Italian Jew.'

'No, I am from England. I am a tourist.'

'So. I too am a tourist, of a kind, from Poland.' She laughed, a little sadly. 'You didn't think I was Jewish when you spoke to me.'

I smiled back, rather uneasily, and then we both laughed.

'Let's go and have some coffee,' I said.

When she laughed freely, all the sadness vanished. We continued to speak in German, but often she would use a Yiddish expression, and when she spoke Yiddish it had all the fruity tang of a complete language, unlike the barbarous mixture that I had heard spoken in our little community at home.

Malcah was her name. First I told her, in my halting German, which part of Russia my parents had come from. It was near enough to the Polish border to make us feel that we had an origin in common, and we laughed at the miracle which brought *landsleit* together in strange places. She found it quite hard to understand the circumstances in which I had come to Florence. 'Your schoolteacher, a Christian *galach*, brought you here, for *nothing*?' I tried to explain the relation of Jew to

Christian in England, but the whole thing seemed unreal to her. And then she told me her own story. In that cheerful café atmosphere, it was a good deal more difficult to understand than my own.

She and a companion, Moshe, had left Poland some days before, *en route* for Palestine, where they were to settle. Having been a student of art at the university, she had jumped at the chance of going through Italy, and they were to make their way to Haifa on a small tramp ship due to sail from the port of Livorno in a few days. So far it all sounded normal, but now began the confusion. For reasons which I could not quite follow, but which had something to do with an immigration quota, Moshe and she were to enter Palestine as man and wife, though they were not married. It soon became clear that months of finagling, a morass of intrigue, lay behind their plans, complicated by the fact that Moshe's father, and Moshe himself, were members in Poland of a political party, some brand of anarchists, I gathered, that was very decisively outlawed in Italy. Moshe could not therefore travel in Italy under his own name, his father being too well known to the police. To meet these various problems—she told it all to me with complete confidence that I would understand perfectly—they had been provided in Poland with two sets of passports, the first being their own individual passports on which they had travelled out of Poland, and the second a joint passport with a false name on which they were to cross Italy, embark on the ship, and enter Palestine.

But Moshe was apparently the world's worst intriguer. It is in the nature of anarchists, of course, to be bunglers—almost their philosophy. Malcah had been carrying the joint passport, 'for safety'. They had arrived at the borders of Italy during the night and somewhat earlier than expected; and Moshe, asked for his passport, had thoughtlessly put his hand into his pocket and produced the wrong one—the passport, that is, which bore his real name. The carabinieri had found this name quickly on their black-list and marched him off for interrogation. Malcah, fortunately, had been standing away from him when it happened. She had presented her own passport when her turn came, had been admitted without trouble, and was now ready to leave. But she was without her 'husband'.

'But why haven't you gone straight on to Livorno, now?' I asked her. 'Aren't you worried?'

'All my life I have wanted to see Florence,' she said. 'This will be my last chance, I am sure. I am staying at an address which Moshe knows. If he does not turn up here, perhaps he will reach Livorno in time. If not . . .' she shrugged her shoulders, 'I will have to see. But I have loved everything in Florence. To be here alone, to wander day after day through the galleries seeing the great masters has meant everything to me.'

This was the hardest thing of all for me to understand, her ability to enjoy Florence with all Sedgewick's calm and devotion while her life was in such confusion. The rest—false passports and police—was perhaps not so extraordinary for a real European. I recalled that my own parents had originally left Russia thirty years earlier on a false passport. It had not been considered very unusual in those days. I suddenly thought also of a story of Cellini's that I had read in his *Memoirs* that week, how, fleeing for his life from the police of this very city, four hundred years earlier, he had disguised himself as a monk with the help of his friend Fra Alesso, and slipped away to Siena under the very noses of the Florentine police. Still, to connect all this with a simple Jewish girl, who might have been my sister or my cousin, sitting beside me drinking coffee, required quite an effort.

It became easier when Malcah told me about her life in Poland, the bitter hatred between Jew and non-Jew, the bloody fights at the university when Jewish students resisted the *numerus clausus* edicts and took whole courses standing rather than sit on the allotted 'yellow badge' benches. She had spent one year studying in Vienna, where she had picked up the student song that I had heard her sing that night, and this was in retrospect the happiest year of her life.

But to her, the tranquil life of an English Jew, and of English students generally, seemed equally mystifying.

'What political party do you belong to?' she asked me.

43

'Oh, I don't know. I suppose I'm a Socialist.'
'Yes, everybody's a socialist. But what *faction?*'
She was puzzled at anyone not wanting to get his position quite clear.
'Have you taken part in many demonstrations?' she wanted to know.
'Well, no. But we do have political debates sometimes.'
'Debates? What do you debate?'
'Oh, I think the last debate we had was on the question whether it was right to execute King Charles.'
'King Charles? When was that? Oh, you mean at the time of Cromwell?' Incredulously, 'You are still debating that?'
We talked on and on. At a café bar, we ordered liqueurs, and raised our glasses to each other with a word that brought us together: '*l'chayim*'. Then I walked her home and said good night.
'Can I help you in any way?' I asked her.
'I don't know. Perhaps. I may still be in trouble. We shall see.'
She gave me a friendly kiss when I left her, and I walked home full of excitement through the quiet streets. I had never been out so late in Florence. Under a scudding moon, all the modern city had dropped into darkness, and only the ancient buildings were left, monumental, and the grey Arno.
We were to meet again on Saturday evening.

★   ★   ★

The Sedgewicks and I went our own ways on Saturday morning, but in the afternoon the Headmaster and I set off for a walk together across the Ponte Vecchio into the Boboli Gardens. As we sat in the flower gardens at the top of the hill, looking across the valley towards San Miniato, the Headmaster talked about the liberation that the Renaissance had brought to the human spirit. I nursed my secret. My mind was on Poland, and perhaps Sedgewick found me inexplicably truculent that afternoon.
'The Renaissance was no liberation for the Jews, you know,'

I told him. 'It was really almost the opposite, a turning point backwards. Before the Renaissance the Jews were more literate than the Christians. They carried Greek learning to the Arabs and Arab learning to the Christians. But at the Renaissance, Christian education went forward and Jewish education retired into a shell for four hundred years. Israel Abrahams says in *Jewish Life in the Middle Ages*: "The Jewish Middle Ages began just when the medieval cloud vanished from Christian society."'

'But surely,' said Sedgewick, 'in Italy the Jews shared in the culture around them, and lived a very full life.'

'Oh, yes, in Italy. But I was thinking of real Jewry, the great masses of Jews in Eastern Europe.'

How could the Head know what was for him unknowable?

I met Malcah late that evening, and we talked again over coffee, and walked happily together, sometimes hand in hand, through the streets and along the Arno bank. We spoke little of Jewish things, much more of our schooldays and studies, exchanging quotations of French or German poetry, humming the themes of music we knew, and most of all talking of novels and novelists, an endless encircling subject. The awkwardness of our first meeting had gone, and we were together and alone, as two wanderers who have met by fate at the top of a mountain.

When I left her at the door of her *pension*, she told me, with great embarrassment, how I could help her.

'Can you lend me some money? I need about a thousand lire to pay my bill here and to get my luggage to Livorno. And I would like to buy some reproductions. I don't know now if Moshe will appear....'

A thousand lire was about ten pounds in real money. Ten pounds was a large sum for me to find, but I said I would have it for her by Tuesday at the latest.

Then, even more shyly, she said: 'Could you travel with me to Livorno? It's not a great distance, but I am somehow a little worried about the police at railway stations. I would feel safer if you could come with me. And it would be nice if we could travel together. You are surely going to Pisa, and that is so close to Livorno.'

I saw that she still had no understanding of my status with the Headmaster—or perhaps she understood him better than I did. 'I would love to,' I said. 'I will try . . . but it is a little hard.'

I wanted desperately to go with her, to carry the whole thing off as a free person would, but what could I tell Sedgewick? To tell him the whole story, in all its simplicity, seemed quite impossible. Then what? I tried out a few far-fetched stories in my head. Should I tell him that I wanted to see the ancient synagogue at Livorno, the oldest in Italy? Should I talk about the famous Jewish scholars of Pisa and Livorno—Raphael Meldola, Azulai, Daniel da Pisa—and see what came up? Could I suggest quite innocently that I thought of going off for a few days alone to explore the country around?

I went into the railway station the next morning, while the Sedgewicks were at church, and sent off a telegram to Arthur, counting every word carefully: 'WIRE TEN POUNDS HOOK CROOK POSTE RESTANTE FLORENCE' and I went back to the hotel, feeling a shadow growing around me.

★ ★ ★

How was it that on Monday morning at breakfast the Headmaster, reading his mail, looked up and said to me:

'Would you like a few days on your own, to trot over to Pisa, and perhaps down to Siena? Some dear friends of ours at Ravenna have asked us if we would motor over to see them for a couple of days, and if you would be quite happy on your own, we would like to. Yes, you must go down to Siena. Aeneas Sylvius's home ground, eh? How you will love it. One should see it, perhaps, for the first time alone. It bursts on one like a thunderclap. What wouldn't I give to see it again for the first time.'

I looked at the Head and Mrs Sedgewick, and the story of Malcah trembled on my lips. Some final block kept it back, some painful relic of Jewish or adolescent self-containment. I

MALCAH AND SEDGEWICK

agreed to their plan, and wondered if they sensed my inner wretchedness.

At the post office, Arthur's telegram was waiting for me with a draft for twelve pounds. Good old Arthur. My spirits rose. When I met Malcah briefly that day I told her that all was well. I would go with her.

As the train pulled out of Florence the next morning, I felt at first an exultant sense of adventure. With a carriage to ourselves we had, for a brief moment, got the better of the world around us. We gave each other a hug of welcome, but then sat silent side by side for a long time, as it seemed, watching the olives and cypresses flash by, and sharing a sadness whose cause was gradually borne in on me. Malcah said nothing, but I knew that she was thinking of the Vienna that she had grown to love, and of her week in Florence, leisurely days of art and beauty that were now over. She had needed me for this last short journey not for protection but to share her nostalgia. I felt it all in the deep silence and in the tears glistening in her eyes. The Europe she loved had rejected her. She would settle and build in Palestine. She would take new root, perhaps win a new freedom. But she had been rejected.

We walked around Pisa, saying little, but happy to be sharing this last breath of Italy. It was a golden day, when walking itself seemed like floating in air. At Livorno all was so normal and orderly that we laughed at the anti-climax. Moshe had been released and had made his own way down to Livorno that very day. He was due back at the ship within an hour. Malcah and I walked along the shore promenade together for a last word before she went on board.

'I will send you the money very soon,' she said.
'I know you will. Don't worry about it.'
We were at the ship's side now.
'Good-bye, Malcah,' I said.

She threw her arms around me, and the tears streamed down her cheeks. I kissed her ardently, and she stumbled up to the ship. Our story was at an end.

Back at school two weeks later, the episode seemed hardly

worth telling, even to Arthur. It had lost its urgency. Three months later, six pounds arrived from Malcah, and three months after that the remaining six pounds. She wrote again to me twice, each time with growing anger at the British: and then there was a long silence.

When I visited Palestine ten years later, I went to see her in the settlement at Kfar Haran, in Galilee, where she lived. But by then I had other things on my mind. I had changed. She had changed. Too much had happened.

Wandering now around the Cathedral Close at Lydford, I preferred to think back to the days in Florence. Good-bye, Malcah. Our story seemed worth telling at last. I have told it now for one who wanted to understand—for Sedgewick.

JONAS, MY OLD FRIEND

I SAT holding Juliet's new novel in my hand and looking out at the London fog; and my mind went back to that August years ago when we were the only two people in New York— a relentless sun, endless martinis in her dark, cool apartment, and *talk*—wry, cheerful talk with our hair down—everyone away, wives, husbands, lovers—no battles to be fought, no positions to be won—a month of looking at each other and smiling at our absurdity. Bit by bit most of our pet stories about ourselves had come out. Sometimes, at least in my case, the comment received wasn't quite as expected. But I could take it. It is so much easier to smile at one's absurdity when fortified by drink. We never met much after that before I returned to England, but when we did it was always wry and pleasant, though never in the same way.

Early in that martini-drenched month she had given me her book on Yeats' last poems. In return I had lent her the still unpublished manuscript of my book on the Midrash, though I never really believed that she could make much of it. How could anyone born in Kansas City of good Baptist stock know what the rabbis had been talking about in the Midrash, two thousand years ago? Not that she had any remote feeling about *her* kind of Jews. Far from it. Settled in New York after a sojourn as a script-writer in Hollywood, she would have said— which was obvious—that Jews were her best friends. They were the sparkle in the champagne, the gherkin that comes with the pastrami sandwich. Life for her would have been infinitely dull without Jews, as presumably life for me would be dull without goyim.

What indeed would I do without goyim? Mustn't the Jews get a bit bored in Israel? Granted that we're all such fun, can't one have too much of a good thing? As for champagne, what's the use of being a bubble without something to bubble in?

But this would mean that a Jew is 'different'. O.K. So be it. *Vive la différence*. Or so, anyhow, it seemed, sitting at ease in a cool New York apartment, looking down happily into a third frosty martini. Perhaps it is not always such fun to be a Jew: but to be the same as everybody else? . . . How *grey*.

When I was a schoolboy, I had an old friend—Jonas—who wanted to end the difference. Or so he said. The Jews had to disappear, in his view, 'without leaving a trace'. The ageless story of suffering should be brought to an end. A Jew must be like everybody else. To say this dispassionately sounds reasonable enough, but to see and hear Jonas saying it gave the game away. He put all the passion of the centuries into it. He was Moses and Isaiah and Trotsky thundering away from Mount Sinai, dashing the tablets of stone into a thousand fragments at his feet. For there was one difference that he insisted on clinging to. The Jews had a special score to settle—with God. God had selected the Jews for his particular anger: every Jew had to fight back—to defy God—to *prove* we were no different. We had our weapon: reason. We should use it.

I had told Juliet about Jonas when she gave me her book on Yeats. It had seemed to me at first that there was a good deal in common between him and Jonas—two old men raging against the dying of the light. But I had soon seen the difference. Yeats was a pagan. The despair of old age to him was his loss of power as a man. *I climb to the tower-top and lean upon broken stone.* Words could bring back the memory of Byzantium, but it was still empty. Without the power to feel, a man had been cheated of life.

This would have been alien to Jonas, as to the rabbis of old. The rabbis had sensed, without always saying it, that man's exultation in his physical power was the fatal weakness of the pagan world around them. If death is not to be a defeat, there must be something in man that stays unconquerable: faith, said some; charity, said others. Jonas, of course, had his own version: defiance.

Juliet had liked the sound of Jonas, but I wonder how he would have liked her novel. It is all about quarrelsome, loose-

JONAS, MY OLD FRIEND

living, self-indulgent people caught in their own trap: a pointless story, it would have seemed to him, a waste of time, perhaps, except possibly in one way: as part of the Great Argument. If one bothered about it at all, he might have said, it showed—as everything shows—that there is no such thing as happiness: there is no inherent beauty or peace in life. But—he would go on—that is only a starting point. One doesn't sit back and let life pass over one as a consequence. If one accepts that life is tragic, one must pin this remorselessly on a cruel, pitiless God: *that* is the way out of the dilemma of living, that together with the ceaseless use of one's reason. *The hammered gold and gold enamelling* . . . if he had heard Yeats's words he would have spewed them out. Art and artifice, beauty and sentiment—it was all a fraud. What is there then? The flame of reason in man. Even God can be singed by argument.

We had endless discussions, sitting in his grim northern hovel. I wish in a way that I could have introduced him to Yeats's poetry. I had got as far as Shelley with him, but some of Yeats's lines would have had the right air of sonority:

> '*All that man is,*
> *All mere complexities,*
> *The fury and the mire of human veins . . .*'

Yes, he would have said, but where is the *defiance*? One doesn't give up because the life-force wanes. That would make man's history an endless succession of weak attempts to stay alive a little longer, and what a contemptible story *that* would be. There is no virtue itself in living, only in living for some purpose. By this standard a short life or a long life have equal value.

And so the argument would proceed, while all around him life gambolled on, full of the petty and pretty ironies that he wanted to override. As Jonas saw it, the centre of his life was a struggle with God. As his friend and neighbour, the little Jewish shopkeeper, Barron, saw it, the real problem was whether this rich, cranky old miser could be persuaded, cajoled or tricked into leaving his money to support the upbuilding of the Land of Israel. It was a lot of fun. Juliet had enjoyed the story, sipping her martini. But as usual she had been ready with her own comment.

* * *

Jonas lived in the small industrial town of Prescott in the north of England, a background that had been specially designed for him by Providence. Today Prescott has spreading suburbs of comfortable small homes and gardens, and even the old back-to-back brick houses in the centre of the town are festooned with television aerials and bursting inside with electric washing machines. But in those days physical comfort was unknown. Prescott was the iron works, the coal-mines linked with them, and a few metal goods factories. My mother had moved there to be close to a widowed sister when my father had gone away to a post in Canada, and at first I had missed the little seaport town in which I had grown up. But Prescott soon took hold of me in its own way.

I had just won the scholarship that took me south to Lydford and Fenner College, so it was only the school holidays that I spent at Prescott. But it was not just the feeling of coming home that made the town so painfully attractive. The moment I got into the train at Euston for the long journey home, a kind of northern excitement would enter me. As the flat green fields of the south rolled by, my mind went forward not so much to the food and warmth of home as to the harsh black hilliness of the world I was coming back to. There would be no one at the station to meet me: meeting at the station was a form of sentiment unknown in my family. I could catch the tram at the station that took me close to my house. And I preferred to greet Prescott alone, to crowd into a rattling tramcar with the shabby cheerful housewives going home laden from the Market Square, jostle with the dour cloth-capped miners in the cobbled streets, and watch the throngs of cheeky-looking girls streaming out of the factory gates. I would breathe it all in, happy to be back. Then would come the first good heavy meal, with all its familiar savours. I would unpack and settle down. I would sleep deeply,

JONAS, MY OLD FRIEND

waking early to the clip-clop of the miners walking to work in their wooden-soled boots. And then, with my feet on the earth and safe in that familiar intimate world, I would feel ready for my meeting with Jonas.

Once I had come to know Jonas as a friend, I would walk up Albert Street to see him in his miserable crowded house on the first afternoon after my return home from school. I felt happy enough just to be walking in the hilly streets, breathing that fresh northern air, after the soft flatness of the south. But it was the talks with Jonas, the endless passionate argument about everything that made my liberation complete. At school we argued too, but the issues there were unreal. We read love poetry that had no relation to our joking about sex. The struggles in history books were about remote issues and remote people. But when I talked to Jonas, it was he and I, arguing in that dismal room, that were the issues, and he staked his life—and mine—on the outcome.

He was never temperate, as the masters were at school, but committed and angry. When I argued with him, I felt that he was pushing his way through some closed door, and that I was helping. Superficially, we were at loggerheads. To Jonas, the world was a vast deception, a cruel plot that man had to outwit. The role that therefore fell to me was to argue that there was, running through all things, an unsullied stream of beauty waiting to be uncovered. I tried to persuade him, whenever he let me speak, that life could really be beautiful if only one made it so. Yet at the same time I rejoiced in his hatred of all such pious platitudes.

In an odd way, when I turned off Market Square up the steep slope of Albert Street towards Jonas's house on Salisbury Terrace, it was almost as if I were going to confession, though in fact it was I who sat silent most of the time, listening to a relentless tale—God's injustice and man's stupidity. But he spoke for me, and I knew it. When he cursed man's fate he spoke for all the obedient schoolboys who learn their lessons conscientiously, are kind to their parents, and ready, when the time comes, to fall into a job with prospects. I always had plenty

53

of arguments ready in my head to trot out, like one of Job's comforters, whenever I could get a word in. But I never wanted to win the argument; and it was almost with a sense of absolution that I would finally walk away from his home.

Thinking of it, I can recover exactly the intense physical happiness of those evening walks from Jonas's house. Prescott itself, as I came down the hill, had a more cheerful air, the harsh brick softened by twilight, the endless rows of mean houses humanized now by the glow of coal fires here and there through the front-room windows. Or perhaps it had a defiant air for me as I strolled down past the opening pubs on Victoria Road, cutting through the corner sheds of the Tonbridge Iron Works, kicking away cheerfully at lumps of coal or empty cans lying around, turning the corner at the tin hut of the Salem Mission towards the respectable, bow-fronted houses of Gladstone Place, and so, past Barron's Clothing Store, into the Market Square again, where flaring kerosene lamps threw an exciting light on the fruit-laden stalls, the Punch and Judy man still held the children open-mouthed with his shrill chatter, and over it all, with smoke filling the heavens, the black clouds glowed with the hot breath of the steel furnaces.

How I loved the restless energy that had created all this. Once there had been gently rolling moors, as there were still, five miles away, with sheep grazing quietly within the stone-fenced fields. Industry, with a demonic urge, had stripped it all bare, yet in so doing had uncovered a fiercer beauty—some hidden bone-structure of power. Dimly I felt that Jonas was part of this. Gaunt and crippled, stripped of all comfort in body and mind, he seemed to draw a special passion out of poverty and ugliness: and some part of me responded.

★ ★ ★

It was ironic that it should all have begun out of Bible lessons. Originally my mother had sent me to him, as my father was away, to make progress in Hebrew. We were to do Bible translation twice a week during the school holidays. Jonas—

JONAS, MY OLD FRIEND

terribly old, lean, stooping, and crippled by gout—was famous among the few Jewish families of Prescott as the town's miser and misanthrope. But they also respected him as their only Hebrew scholar, his father having been a rabbi in Lithuania. He gave me lessons without charge, and even in those early days we seemed to be helping each other in a special way. He had never before had to consider the Bible in English, and the archaic language of the Authorized Version fascinated him. Sometimes we would find different things in the same text. I remember reading first the Hebrew and then the English of one lovely verse from the Psalms:

> '*With the sound of my own grief, my bones*
> *cleave to my skin;*
> *I am like a pelican in the wilderness,*
> *like an owl in the desert;*
> *I wait alone, like a sparrow on the*
> *housetop....*'

When the words were out, we sat musing over them silently, I surprised to hear the sound of nature in the middle of a Hebrew lesson, he suddenly conscious, perhaps, of the deep anguish of his enemy the Psalmist.

For the Psalmist, and Isaiah, and Jeremiah and the others were all his personal enemies. As I grew older, we still started the lessons with a chapter or two of Hebrew, moving from the Psalms to Job or Ecclesiastes—but much more we would just sit and talk. Once he saw that I was old enough to struggle, he seemed to feel that I was fair game. To translate Hebrew was a legitimate exercise, even, in some ways, an enjoyable one. But to *believe* in what the words said, to take it sanctimoniously—this was an outrage, and he would tell me why, in his fierce, guttural English.

Any subject would do to start off his anger, but in the end every argument came back to God and his peculiar creation, the Jewish people. That Jews, suffering everywhere and through all the ages, should praise God for their existence seemed to him not merely absurd but monstrous: the primeval sin. Were Jews supposed to take a special pride in being the victims of God's so-called love? No. Pride lay in protesting against it. It was evil to prolong this two-thousand-year story of suffering. There was only one way in which we Jews could still fool God. We could split up, merge, disappear without leaving a trace. This was the first step towards getting even with God's long list of triumphs against us.

'Isn't it simple reason?' he would say. Everything, and particularly every sentimentality, had to be held up and weighed by pitiless, humourless reason. I would pay dearly for a vague remark such as: 'I like Wordsworth.' He would want chapter and verse, and I would have to produce a text and read. In that grim background, the love of nature did indeed sound absurd. He would listen intently, ready to pounce, nodding occasionally at a sententious line—*the world is too much with us*—but through most of it—*trailing clouds of glory, pansies at my feet*—grimacing horribly. I remember that when I told him I had started to study economics at school he asked me to explain it, and that when I talked, fresh from my first lessons, about 'the laws of supply and demand' he lost all patience.

'You waste your time on this,' he shouted, 'when there are men crawling on their stomachs in the mines to hack out a ton of coal, coming home, night after night, to the same misery and poverty! Have you seen them in their hovels, in this very street? Have you seen them in the public houses, stupefying themselves with beer to forget the horrible pit they work in? Is this another God-given law, supply and demand? Is this God's love of mankind . . . ?' and we were back again to his favourite subject.

I couldn't be flippant. It was the worst sin. I remembered that once, when he had said impatiently that I was 'too young and childish' to understand what I was saying, I had tried to tease him—and probably to show off—by quoting some verses from the Wisdom of Solomon:

> '*For honourable old age is not that which standeth in length of time,*
> *Nor is its measure given by number of years,*
> *But an unspotted life is ripe old age. . . .*'

JONAS, MY OLD FRIEND

Far from smiling, he had burst into another torrent. 'What is this supposed to mean? *An unspotted life!* To be innocent is good? What is innocence? Just a form of ignorance. Is this the wisdom of Solomon? How can an intelligent person be taken in by all this rubbish?'

Yet he spent all his time arguing about this sort of 'rubbish'. It was as if, in some perverse way, he agreed with the old rabbi who had said of the Bible: *Turn it over and over again, for in it is everything.*

★ ★ ★

I never discovered what there was in Jonas's history that had so embittered him. It seemed not his personal condition but the wastefulness of suffering that he found enraging.

His miserliness reflected this. It actually hurt him to spend money carelessly, just as it hurt him to accept any belief without counting the cost. Yet he was undoubtedly very rich. Coming to England as a young man, he had worked as a travelling peddler until, after years of saving, he had acquired some money and begun to buy cheap houses. By the time I knew him, he owned a vast amount of slum property in Prescott, all administered with scrupulous avarice. He lived himself in one of the worst of his own houses, surrounded on all sides by tenants who hated him and whose children jeered in the street at the crooked, shambling figure who came weekly to collect the rents.

Once he must have been tall, but when I knew him he was already bent double with age and pain. Yet one could still see dignity in his high forehead and long straight nose; and though his fingers were twisted by gout into gargoyle shapes, they were immensely long and expressive.

I used to think his hands were beautiful, twisted as they were. I was always looking in those days for beauty shining through the ugliness around us. Perhaps this was why it was always a relief to me when I ran into Mrs Maclean, his housekeeper, who lived upstairs with her little daughter, Mary. Jonas had been married, but his wife had died in childbirth, the child dying too. Mrs Maclean had looked after him for years—spruce, buxom and as appetizing as fresh-baked scones. When she saw me in the hall, she would greet me with a Scottish burr of welcome. If, when I knocked at the door, Mary opened it, the sight of this child—lithe and raven-haired—would be like some soft chord of beauty. But this was uncommon. Jonas lived in the hideously crowded front-room facing the street, and he usually saw me coming and opened the door himself.

Once inside, I had left my schoolboy world. The room was crowded with ancient Victorian rubbish, all bought at auctions. Jonas usually lay on a huge rusty old bed, while I sat in a squeaky rocking chair. Books of all kinds littered the floor, often still tied up in their 'penny bundles'. There was even a decrepit harmonium up against one wall, and occasionally I heard him trying to play it. It was a sound of agony, almost as if a lost soul, imprisoned in the room, were crying out for release.

★ ★ ★

Jonas had almost nothing to do with the Jewish families of Prescott. Whenever a collection was made for a Jewish charity, the leaders of the small community had been wont to call on him, only to emerge baffled with a gift of a shilling or one and sixpence. It became gradually established that the only man to visit him for such collections was little Joe Barron, who owned the successful clothing-store in the Market Square and devoted himself to good works. Dapper, innocent, and irrepressibly cheerful, Barron could not really believe that Jonas meant all the wicked things he said; and in a curious return, Jonas treated Barron with a kind of amused tolerance. They came from towns close to each other in the old country, and perhaps this was some link.

Even Barron rarely succeeded in extracting much money for charity, but he continued to call, unperturbed. Jonas was reputed to have said kind words about the work of hospitals—medical science was after all one of man's ways of outwitting

JONAS, MY OLD FRIEND

God's malevolence—and Barron hoped that Jonas might give money one day to a Jewish hospital, perhaps even a Jewish hospital in Palestine—a double *mitzvah*. Jonas gave him no encouragement: he thought Zionism quite reactionary. But no rebuffs could keep Barron down, and when they met he even managed to make Jonas smile sometimes with stories of old times.

When I was there alone, though, the argument was entirely different in tone. I would give him a cigarette, which he broke into two—half to be kept for smoking later—and we were arguing instantly. In the early days I had just listened while he framed an endless protest in terms of his own world—'Why did man suffer so? Where was the power for good?'—but gradually, as my own reading broadened, I found myself feeding his argument with ideas from the outside, a world he hardly knew. Yet though it was I who brought in the new names, the passion and the argument always became his own, and never far from the primitive anger of Job or the cynicism of Ecclesiastes.

I could never tell in advance who would appeal to him. When I discovered Spinoza, I thought that this might be his mark—a Jew rejected and then reclaimed by the Jews—ethics without the trimmings. But Jonas found him worse than Isaiah.

'Do you think he has freed himself?' he said bitterly. 'He's still afraid of God. Why should there be a "God" imminent in everything? Why doesn't he just call it "natural law"? And how can he pretend that there is no such thing as absolute evil? There *is*, the world is full of it. . . .' and so to his usual harangue.

I did no better with Schopenhauer. This time, the pessimism was too unrelieved. Was Jonas indeed a pessimist at all? He saw some good in the virtues of simple people. There was joy in the struggle against a capricious God.

When I saw this, I realized suddenly that he was, after all, a romantic, and I tried Shelley on him, with instant success; not the lyrics, but *Prometheus Unbound*. Extended on his rusty bed, he saw himself chained to the rock—and he loved the pomposity of the diction:

MEMOIRS OF A SPECIAL CASE

'Fiend, I defy thee! With a calm fixed mind
All that thou canst inflict I bid thee do;
Foul Tyrant, both of God and Human-kind,
One only being shalt thou not subdue.'

He marked every protest in the copy I lent him. And one line he underscored heavily: *'I wish no living thing to suffer pain.'*

* * *

Now Barron had a daughter, and, as the Bible would say, Barron's daughter was surpassing fair. She was, in fact, fair in more than the Biblical sense. She actually had blue eyes and golden hair, which to me had a peculiar appeal. I found myself spending more and more time in her house in the intervals of visiting Jonas; and here, from little Joe Barron, bursting with energy and goodwill, I began to be subjected to a different kind of pressure. It was my duty, according to Barron, to help bring Jonas back to the Jewish community. The reason was simple. The Zionist societies of northern England were in sharp rivalry. Fossbridge had raised nearly £2,000 that year against Prescott's miserable £800; and Abe Levi, the chairman at Fossbridge, was crowing. In Singleton, only twenty miles away, the local rich man had left £5,000 to the Jewish National Fund in his will. Prescott had to do something, and I, as the intimate of Jonas—almost like his son—was the person to help. Jonas was a sick man. What about his will? What good would his money do him when he had gone? After all, Jonas was the son of a rabbi and a Hebrew scholar, and Zionism was the only way of keeping the Jewish people alive. . . . Through all this I would sit looking dreamily at Betty Barron, wondering how soon I could politely get her out of the house for a walk in the park.

Perhaps I was already getting a little weary of Jonas. I still went for lessons, but there was always now the thought that soon I would be seeing Betty. The park, with its short steep terraces looking out towards the distant steel mills, was our private paradise. How I loved those walks, and how exquisitely I suffered when we arranged to meet there at night—which was forbidden—and she was late. There was one night—the most wonderful torture of all—when she never came. We had quarrelled: she said she wouldn't come, but I went all the same. Oh, those cold empty hours of waiting—the hard black asphalt paths, the sooty leaves, the flowerless earth. I went home miserable: but the next day we fell into each other's arms and all was well again.

It was all fairly innocent, but not, I soon learnt, to Jonas. We were reading the Book of Job one day when he broke off suddenly with a wildly unexpected question.

'Tell me,' he said, 'do you ever think of marriage? Do you plan what you will do?'

'Well no,' I said laughing. 'It's a little early for that, isn't it?'

'Barron was here yesterday,' said Jonas, 'pestering me with his Zionist nonsense. He tells me that you are often in his house, and that you see a lot of his daughter, Betty. Is she a special friend of yours?'

'Of course,' I said warmly. 'She's very nice. I like her very much.'

'But you wouldn't *marry* her, would you?' said Jonas. 'You wouldn't marry *any* Jewish girl?'

'Why not?' I said. 'Why shouldn't I, if I wanted to and she agreed?'

'Why not! A young man with your intelligence, going to study at Oxford University, asks such a question! You know history, you know what has happened to the Jewish people. How could you bear to bring any more Jews into the world?'

Now I could see it. We were back at the old stand.

'But my mind doesn't work that way,' I said. 'Surely a person must be free to follow any of his desires. No one should be forbidden to marry anybody else, either because she's Jewish or because she's non-Jewish.'

'Oh, my poor friend,' cried Jonas, 'how can I make you understand! It's the *principle* that's important above everything else. One must live by principle. To live by whim, by pleasure, leads to chaos. Listen to me. You're too young to marry now anyway, but perhaps this will make you understand. You know that I don't like to throw money away—that's a principle too. But I will give you a hundred pounds the day you marry a Christian girl. One hundred pounds. Now do you see what I mean?'

'A hundred pounds! That's a lot of money. I'll have to start looking quickly before you change your mind. . . .'

I tried to talk jokingly, but for the first time I felt somehow sickened by Jonas. When I left that day, I met Mrs Maclean outside the door with Mary. They looked so clean and wholesome after the kind of argument that went on in the room below them. Mary was growing into a tall and strikingly handsome girl. Looking at her dark intense beauty, her long straight nose, her high forehead, I suddenly wondered about their relation to Jonas. Mrs Maclean was smiling her usual greeting, but there was something of an anxious look in her eyes.

'He's not been well, you know,' she said. 'He worries so, sitting up half the night studying those big Hebrew books of his.' She sighed. 'He's such a *good* man,' she said. 'I do wish he'd take more care of himself. He's not at all strong, you know.' I had never had such a long conversation with her. I went away very puzzled. But the holidays were over now. I was on my way to my first term at Oxford.

★ ★ ★

With Oxford, everything changed. Prescott suddenly began to fade. Away at last from school, away from home, away from Prescott, I pulled an iron curtain up around me to make doubly sure that nothing got through. In my first holiday at Christmas I met my mother briefly in London and then went abroad as a tutor in a French family until term began again. I had lost touch with Betty. She, too, had left home, to train as a nurse in Leeds. Writing to her had not really worked. I had too much to say: she had too little We had been better walking hand-in-hand in the park, where words were unimportant.

JONAS, MY OLD FRIEND

And then one day in February, with the second term well advanced, I got a telegram from Joe Barron: '*Come immediately: Jonas very ill.*' I took a train that same afternoon and was in Prescott late at night. I went home quickly to see my mother, and leaving my bag there hurried round to Joe Barron's.

'He's terribly ill,' Barron said. 'He's been ill for months, but last week, with all this damp and fog, he had a very serious attack. It's very bad. I saw him this morning and the doctor says there's no hope.'

'Did he ask for me?' I said.

'His mind's going,' Barron said. 'But when I mentioned you, he smiled. I'm sure he would want to see you. And it's very important. You can help us. Perhaps you're the only one who can help. Do you know what it is? I saw his lawyer, Mr Andrews. He told me that Jonas had left instructions: he doesn't want to be buried in a Jewish cemetery. He doesn't want to be buried at all. He wants to be cremated—*cremated*—and his ashes to be scattered.

I looked at Barron blankly. "And you want me . . .'

'Of course,' Barron said. 'You must talk him out of this nonsense. . . .'

'But why shouldn't he . . .'

'Why *shouldn't* he? A Jew: a Jewish scholar: the son of a rabbi—not to be buried in holy ground. . . .'

'But you *know* he never believed . . .'

'What do you mean *believed*? A Jew is free to do what he likes when he lives, but when he dies he goes back to his people. . . .'

'But if he doesn't want to?'

'How can *he* know what he wants? The man is dying. His mind is confused. We must bring him back. He won't even see the rabbi: a very good rabbi I brought over specially from Leeds yesterday. . . .'

'Why don't you all leave him alone?' I said bitterly. 'You want him to leave some money for Palestine, I suppose. . . .'

Barron smiled tolerantly. 'Now that's quite another matter. Let's not worry about that just now. But he *must* see the rabbi.

63

Perhaps you can persuade him. Remember,' he said firmly, 'he really wants to come back now. You can help him.'

I left Barron and set off up Albert Street. Mary opened the door—a different Mary, ripening to a more delicate beauty. The house was different too. Jonas had been moved upstairs. He had passed completely into Mrs Maclean's care. To me the house had always been Jonas's bedroom on the ground floor, full of books and confusion and argument, with some other rooms elsewhere. Now it had ceased to be Jonas's house at all. He was a lodger, in a big brass bed upstairs. The house was clean-swept, smelling of soap.

Jonas had changed, too. Perhaps it was seeing him lying there in a quiet, clean room that made him seem so different. He was more shrunken than before, and part of the strain, the desperate effort to prove his case, seemed gone. A smile almost of tenderness shone in his eyes when he saw me.

With an immense effort he said: 'I am glad you came,' and laid his bony, twisted hand on mine. Mrs Maclean was in the room quietly tidying up. He motioned to her to come to the bedside and said to me faintly: 'You know, every Jew has two ministering angels. Mrs Maclean and Mary are mine.' I stayed a little while and went downstairs, bewildered and sad.

Mary was in the sitting-room below, Jonas's old room, cleared up and transformed. She smiled at me wanly. 'Everything's changed,' I said. She nodded, but there was nothing more to say.

I came again early the next day, but Barron was there ahead of me, talking anxiously to Mrs Maclean. Jonas was much worse when I went upstairs, and we sat for a few minutes saying nothing. Finally I asked him the question that Barron had insisted I put to him: would he not see the rabbi? He frowned and shook his head, but then whispered: 'Get a Bible.' I ran downstairs and rummaged in a cupboard full of books, Barron hanging over me, pestering me with questions, childishly excited at what had happened. I heard him following me quietly when I went back upstairs with the Bible, though he had the grace to stay outside. Jonas was lying still, and I stood there uncertainly.

Then I saw his lips beginning to move, and leaned over to catch what he was saying. They were faint Hebrew words, but very familiar to me—a chapter of Job. I turned quickly to the passage, and in a strong voice began reading it to him, as I had so often in the past:

> *My soul is weary of my life: I will leave my complaint upon myself: I will speak in the bitterness of my soul.* . . .
> *Is it good unto Thee that Thou shouldst oppress, that Thou shouldst despise the work of Thy hands, and shine upon the counsel of the wicked?*
> *Are not my days few? Cease then, and let me alone.* . . .

I read on, sharing his defiance. He was holding on: he would not give in:

> *Cease then, and let me alone, that I may take comfort a little before I go where I shall not return.* . . .
> *A land of darkness, as darkness itself: and of the shadow of death, without any order, and where the light is as darkness.* . . .

Something in the sonorous Hebrew words held me, and I looked down at him. His lips were no longer moving. The tears ran slowly down his yellow lined cheeks: his youth, his promise and this arid isolation. I fell silent too, and touched his hand in farewell.

I was crying when I went outside. Barron, waiting for me on the landing, took my hands between his and pressed them tight. He had heard the sound of Hebrew without understanding a word, and was satisfied. 'It will be all right,' he said when we got downstairs. 'He has come back to his people. . . .'

'He has *not*,' I said fiercely. 'He has not given in. I *know* what he meant. He . . .'

'Now then,' Barron said comfortingly. 'Don't be upset. Everything will be all right. You will see.'

Jonas died that day. I was with Barron when the news came. He had been to see Andrews again, and there was no question of changing the instructions: cremation, without a service, and the ashes to be scattered. Jonas would disappear, as he wanted to, without leaving a trace. I had expected Barron to be downcast at his defeat, but somehow he was not uncheerful.

'Yes, he was a strange man,' he said. 'But to leave a good Jewish name, that is everything.'

'And Jonas has left a good Jewish name?'

'Oh yes,' Barron said. 'God finds many ways. . . .'

I had a sudden intuition. 'You mean he's left his money to Zionism?'

'Oh no,' Barron said. 'Andrews told me today. He's left a lot of money: the property alone will be worth twenty or thirty thousand pounds. But not a penny to a Jewish cause.'

'But you seem quite happy about it?'

'Happy I'm not,' Barron said. 'But things have a way of working out. God has many ways. You know how he left his money? A hundred pounds to Prescott Hospital—well that's very fine. And the rest? To Mrs Maclean and Mary. The entire estate. She'll be very rich.'

But he was smiling, and I must have looked puzzled.

'She's a very fine woman,' Barron said comfortably. 'I've been talking to her since I heard. She told me that she wants to do something in memory of Jonas—something big. I told her what the Jews are doing in Palestine, and she thinks he was such a learned man, with so many Hebrew books, that he would have liked to have some memorial there. So she's giving us a thousand pounds to establish a bed in his name in the Hadassah Hospital in Jeruslaem. A thousand pounds for certain: perhaps she will give more. Perhaps two thousand pounds. *The Abraham Jonas Bed.* A permanent memorial. Isn't that a very fine thing?'

★ ★ ★

'Why, the old skinflint!' Juliet said, when I told her. 'He never left you a red cent—or, as I believe you British say, a bean.'

'Now honestly, Juliet,' I began. . . .

'Oh, come off it,' she said, pouring out another martini. 'Obviously you expected it. Treated you like a son and all that. . . . Say: what about the daughter, Mary? You obviously assumed

JONAS, MY OLD FRIEND

she was his. Why didn't you offer to marry her? An heiress! Lacking in initiative, my boy.'

'You have no reverence, do you?' I said. 'I suppose that's why I like you.'

'That's why you liked Jonas,' she said. 'He was a good man. Wouldn't take yes for an answer.'

'No, he wouldn't,' I said. 'Took me quite a time to understand. I thought that in all the argument he was looking for a recipe for man's happiness. Of course I got it all upside down....'

It had come to me first in the train, on the way back to Oxford. Jonas had never expected an answer to his questions. There are no answers. And suddenly I had seen that happiness—the easy formula—might be just as irrelevant for young me as for old him. It was a prickly feeling.

It was my first moment of realizing that I was alone in the world, and that every human being is alone. Torn from the excitement of living, I sat there, watching the world spin past, and knowing that I was on my own, and that there was no hope except in that knowledge.

If one has ever heard this music, one's ear stays attuned to it. Some listen for a still small voice. Jonas heard it coming out of a whirlwind.

Poor old Jonas, surrounded by confusion. He hardly knew what he was listening for except that it was more important than everything else in life. Something told him that he must shy away from everything safe and comfortable if his mind was to stay free.

I knew the epitaph that suited him. It was from that same *Wisdom of Solomon* that he had once derided. But there was no tombstone to carve it on. He had seen to that.

I showed Juliet the passage, and she approved:

> For there is in wisdom a spirit full of understanding,
> Clear in utterance, unpolluted, distinct, unharmed,
> All-powerful, all-surveying,
> And penetrating through all spirits that are quick of understanding. . . .

'Not bad,' she said. 'Not bad at all.'

But it wasn't really right. It sounds far too parsonical, wrapped up in Biblical language. How can I make it sound dissident, dissatisfied, disturbing, uncomfortable, forever restless?

THE WORDS AND THE MUSIC

ONE of the biggest changes that struck me after I got back to England was the readiness with which people were prepared to go to Spain for holidays—even middle-aged people who had lived through the thirties as young men and women and felt the fight against Franco to be the central issue of their lives. I suppose that living abroad I had kept a number of my ideas about social attitudes frozen, as the British did who emigrated to the Colonies, dressing religiously for dinner and opening a six-weeks-old *Times* every morning with a flourish. At home, obviously one can't be as rigid as this. Life goes on; and after all holidays are much cheaper in Spain—so off they went, in their droves.

Even Arthur joined in the throng. I say 'even Arthur' because when I had last talked of Spain to him he had been on the point of going there for a different reason—to fight in the International Brigade. He had rung me up at the time to ask about the climate because he knew that I had been to Spain two years earlier; and now here he was ringing me up again, without a blush, to ask if I had any advice to offer.

'We're flying to Gib in a couple of weeks,' he said, 'and renting a car there to tour Andalusia. I remember that you spent a holiday there, didn't you, in the thirties? Wondered if you could give us some tips about places to see.'

'Oh, it must have changed completely since I was there,' I said. 'I don't really remember much about it. I expect the trains run on time now, and it's probably quite prosperous, with the American bases.'

'Oh, Spain doesn't change,' Arthur said. 'Things come and go, but the real Spain is probably just the same.'

He may have been right on this. It was probably because my memory of Spain was fixed on a year of swift change that I was not taking the long view. I had gone there at a moment in history when something miraculous seemed to be happening, both to the Spaniards and the Jews. But history had turned upside down, or perhaps had turned back to normal....

It was hard to forget. There were constant echoes for me. Just that day I had read in the papers that Morocco—now independent—had concluded an arrangement to let the Moroccan Jews resume their emigration to Israel. I thought of the Jews from Marrakesh and Safi whom I had met on my visit to Spain and wondered if they were now going to Israel—assuming, that is, that they had survived the anti-Jewish riots of a few years earlier. Nothing stood still, it was clear, except one's memories.

But there was no need to be gloomy. It had really been a wonderful junket, even if history had only been playing a practical joke on us. The year was 1935 and I had gone to Spain precisely because the invitation was so bizarre. The Government of Spain—the tremblingly young Republican Government—had been struggling desperately to show the world that they had really thrown off the reactionary past. As part of the proof they had announced to the world that in April of that year they would put on, in Cordova, a fiesta for the Jews, to celebrate the 800th anniversary of the birth there of the Jewish philosopher Maimonides. How can one explain what a celebration of this kind meant to a young Jew conscious of history? Spain to a Jew was the land of the Golden Age—and the land of the Inquisition. Had the moment now come when all these ancient quarrels could be resolved? Was there something in the air of Spain—the new Spain—which would let us breathe easily now—there and everywhere?

Not everybody, perhaps, would have felt this way, but Jewish life and Jewish history—two separate things—had not yet come together for me. As a very small boy, in a dreamy little seaport town at the mouth of the Tyne, Jewish life had been my family happiness. As I grew older and read books, Jewish history had become a baffling complex of pride and fear. In Spain above all I had felt the drama at its most intense—the Jewish poets and scholars, the merchants, the nobles, the craftsmen, the fine ladies—*and the Expulsion*. Would I ever find a key to this mystery? And now, in this graceful gesture by Spain, I seemed to see a dream coming true.

Was it only my own dream? Surely, I felt, it was the Spanish dream, too—to burst out of their Bourbon chains, and feel at ease again with all their past. Spanish history had come to life: old memories were being stirred, old scars were being looked at wonderingly by the patient struggling to his feet. Was there any scar in Spanish history like this one? What Spaniard would not feel in those years a great curiosity to see again, with unclouded eyes, some members of that strange people who had dramatized, merely by existing, the paradox and loneliness of Spain; whose memory was burnt into the Spanish consciousness in language and proverb, in pride and guilt; whose love for Spain had been too disturbing to be accepted, too intimate to be wholly shuffled off. History would tell every Spaniard who could listen that the Jews were his other self.

Or was I reading all this into it for my own reasons? Even I, longing to believe, could sense uncertainty in the air. The Republic had run through its first rapture. The graceful gesture toward the Jews of the world was like the wave of a hand from a train passing through a country station. The passengers on the train are not quite sure of the name of the station; the country folk watching the train wave happily in return, but they do not belong on it, and they have no idea where it is going.

* * *

I had called at the Spanish embassy in London before leaving for Cordova, to ask if there were any special facilities for delegates to the celebration. I was going as a half-official visitor from Oxford, where I had just begun to teach. A grand diplomatic *señor* who received me knew nothing at first of any Jewish philosopher or any celebration. He disappeared to inquire, and then returned to the room bursting with courtesies and pride. He hadn't recognized my pronunciation of the philosopher's name. *His* pronunciation was much more elaborately Spanish—*Mai-mō-nides*. 'Of course,' he assured me. 'There are reduced train fares in Spain, reduced hotel rates, free admission to all museums. We shall help you in any way possible. Ah, the great Spanish philosopher Mai-mō-nides.'

So Maimonides—Rabbi Moses ben Maimon—was a Spaniard. I suddenly felt, as I was to feel later in another connection, the inadequacy of all these tight categories. The *Rambam* as we call him—running the initials of his Hebrew name together—was not a Spaniard. He was an Arab Jew, the way I am an English Jew, and my father was a Russian Jew. We had remembered him better than the Spaniards had. I could hear my father reciting every morning the *Rambam*'s 'Thirteen Articles', each beginning with the devout words '*Ani ma'amin be'emunah shlemah*—I believe with perfect faith....' It was hard to think of the *Rambam* as a Spaniard.

Yet the Spaniards had felt some need to claim him for themselves, not because he could be fitted, with his calm humanism, into the death-obsessed fanaticism of the Spanish tradition, but precisely as an offset to their tradition, to help them see why it had developed the way it had against all the impulses of Western life. Maimonides, the Arab Jew, was the Europe they had bypassed. They had persecuted the Jews, burnt them, expelled them, yet in some way they now had to take a position in relation to them.

Did they understand this, and that other thing which my father would have felt, and which I felt? In the dark struggle then taking shape in Europe, *Spain* was the one word which balanced emotionally with *Germany*. In the long story of *Galuth* or exile, the experience in Spain stood separate in Jewish memory—a golden age of poetry and learning which had never found its equal. To bring the Jews back to Spain if only for a celebration was to make every Jew who heard of it feel, for a second, a surge of faith in history. Even with Hitler in the wings, all was not lost.

* * *

I entered Spain through its English gate at Gibraltar, and

looked up an old friend there, Dickie Fothergill, who had been with me at Oxford and was now a naval lieutenant. We had a drink together and he offered to drive me round to see the country. But I had no patience to linger, and said that I would spend more time with him on my return.

In half an hour I was in the Malaga bus, *en route* for Cordova. For company I had with me Borrow's *Bible in Spain* open on my lap. I would read a page or two—'A Night with a Brigand'— 'A Prince of the Gypsies'—and then I would look out of the window dreamily at the same stony hills, the primitive inns, the dark peasants whom Borrow had wandered among a hundred years earlier.

At the bus station in Cordova, the first thing I saw was a large coloured poster advertising a bullfight that was to be held that week at the Cordova arena 'in honour of the 800th birthday of the great Spanish philosopher, scientist, and doctor Maimonides.' All the dignitaries of the area—the governor of the province, the mayor of Cordova, and many others with grandiose titles— had given the fight their patronage. Spain was paying its tribute.

As I wandered through the town in the evening, I saw the poster again in several places, only half-legible in the twinkling street lights, but still brave with its gaudy lettering and proud black bull. There were curious groups of foreigners in the street, obvious visitors to the celebration; and after the first look at each other, we were soon exchanging greetings in various languages.

We were all kin, yet as different as the nations we now belonged to. The French Jews seemed spare in build, neatly dressed, and, with their closely trimmed moustaches, like so many editions of André Maurois. There were Greek Jews, small, dark, and eager, their brown eyes darting everywhere, taking everything in. From Yugoslavia, from Italy—we knew each other and were happy to meet. The company grew, and we sat down at a café in the main street. Up and down the young Spaniards took their traditional evening stroll, the men and girls in separate groups, laughing and teasing each other in their ritual parade. A Palestinian joined us—an English Jew who had left his native land in 1920 to settle in Palestine as a professor of philosophy. It pleased us when he spoke a few words in modern Hebrew, rare in those days outside Palestine. It seemed to make more vivid the peculiar miracle we were sharing.

We were delighted, too, with another visitor, Don José. Small, dapper, and bursting with good spirits, he had started life as Yossilé Shapiro in a small Lithuanian town, had solidified later in Germany into *Herr Doktor* Josef Shapiro, and now, as a refugee living in Madrid, had been translated into Don José de Shapiro. He knew everything, everybody, every language. He was fully adjusted to his new life, and doubtful where he would be next year. He told delightful jokes in Yiddish.

When the party broke up, I wandered off with the Palestinian professor—my erstwhile compatriot—to the river, where the great stone mosque, with its towers and glorious arched doorways, faced the graceful pillars of the old Roman bridge. We stood in silence for a while, enjoying the beauty of the night.

'I suppose Maimonides walked here as a boy,' I said finally. 'Perhaps he watched them building the mosque.'

The professor had a way of smiling ironically before he spoke. 'How pleasant to meet a romantic,' he said. 'Shall I shatter illusions, or would you prefer to keep them?'

'Oh, you mean the dates are wrong,' I said.

'The dates, and a few other things. The great Caliph who built the mosque died in 961. Fifty years later, the mob rose, slaughtered all the Jews they could find, and forced the rest to flee for their lives. The few that were left here were confined to a ghetto. That was the world that Maimonides was born into in 1135.'

'But the Golden Age had not really ended,' I said.

He smiled. 'There were so many Golden Ages, with the Moors and with the Christians. Too many, really. All too short. Most of the Jews would have settled for one long *tin* age if they had had a choice. They didn't have a choice.'

'But how did so much come out of Spain—Maimonides, Moses Ibn Ezra, and the rest—while nothing came out of countries like England?'

THE WORDS AND THE MUSIC

'Nothing out of England? Come, come. *I* came out of England. All part of the same thing, you know.'

'The same thing?'

He was still smiling. 'Oh, yes. That's the beauty of it. The real International, you know. The scholars go on working whatever happens around them. The Arabs rescued Greek philosophy. The Jews picked it up in Arabic, translated it into Hebrew, and passed it on into Latin for the Scholastics. And it goes on, you know. After all, we've learnt something in England, and we're passing it on again in Hebrew in Palestine. We're a strange people, aren't we?'

★ ★ ★

We were all up early in the morning for the opening ceremonies in the city hall. Flags were flying, a band in gay uniform played cheerfully in the square, and as we filed in, rather hesitantly, towards the large hall, we found our hosts—courteous, stately, with long El Greco faces—waiting to greet us. In the hall itself the seats were crowded with Spaniards, except for a number of rows in front reserved for the visitors. An elaborately printed programme was put into our hands. The first morning was to be devoted simply to the official welcome. On the Spanish side the speakers were to be some high officials from Madrid and Cordova. For the visitors there was to be one main speech, by someone I had not seen before—the Chief Rabbi of Belgrade.

I looked at the rabbi standing quietly on the platform—tall, black-bearded, calm. He had waited many centuries for this moment, and would wait again if need be. When the Christian conquest of Spain had been sealed in 1492 by the expulsion of the Jews, some who thought to temporize had stayed behind, waiting for the Inquisition. The others had set out in small boats, and those who survived the journey had found homes in Salonika and Yugoslavia and other lands of the Eastern Mediterranean. There they went on speaking the Spanish of the fifteenth century, singing Spanish folk songs, and remembering the old country.

75

Through the long mellifluous speeches that opened the proceedings, the audience kept their eyes on the tall figure with the black beard. It was nearly one o'clock when he finally rose. When he began to speak in Spanish, slowly, with perfect yet archaic diction, a shudder of recognition seemed to go through the hall. This was their past speaking to them, a past embalmed for nearly five hundred years. No one moved or breathed. He spoke of history and suffering and pride, and as he came to the end his voice rose to the peroration. '*Viva!*' he cried. 'Long live the love that binds men and women to the soil of their ancestors! Long live the faith that burns in all our hearts! Long live the pity that opens men's eyes to God! Long live the country that sheltered us and the land to which we have returned! Long live Cordova the beautiful! Long live Spain!'

He stood silent, and the audience too was stunned into silence. Then in a moment they were all on their feet, clapping, shouting, smiling. The mayor walked over to the rabbi and took both his hands in his. The audience applauded still louder, until finally the mayor raised his hand for silence. 'And now,' he said, 'we beg our distinguished visitors to honour us at a little refreshment we have prepared for them.' The doors at the side of the hall were flung open, and we moved hungrily towards the heavily laden tables.

★   ★   ★

The moment of truth suddenly exploded into a moment of farce. The rabbi was escorted to the table by two distinguished Spaniards. We were all close behind. The waiters, in some elaborate sixteenth-century costume, were bearing down on us carrying huge silver trays on which stood crystal goblets of wine. But in front of us, consternation had broken out. The Spaniards, once again seeking the highest compliment in their power, had prepared a magnificent banquet of shellfish, bringing the lobsters, crabs, shrimps, and other delicacies from Malaga. Alas! It was five hundred years since they had dealt officially with Jews. Perhaps they had some vague notion that the Jews ob-

THE WORDS AND THE MUSIC

jected to eating meat with Christians and had therefore settled for fish. But no one had told them that religious Jews do not eat shellfish or even drink non-Jewish wine. The rabbi had taken one look and fallen back, as if the mere sight of this unclean food would defile him. The visitors around him also shook their heads. To such Jews among us who might well have enjoyed the food at a Spanish restaurant, it became unthinkable to let down the rabbi and his following. We stood around and talked politely for a time while our hosts played with the delicacies and washed them down with wine. Finally we got away.

The ice of the centuries had been broken, and for the rest of the fiesta everything worked with utmost smoothness. Even the bullfight the next afternoon, which might have been expected to pose some problems, passed off with reasonably good humour. It was too early in the season for the real thing. The fight was little more than a testing of bulls, a gay frolic in which the experts pricked and prodded the young animals to find out which of them had enough spirit to fight for their lives on another day. There were moments of discomfort, when the rabbis and the other visitors wished themselves elsewhere, but for the most part they were able to see the thing through. The Jews and the Spaniards were for the moment at peace.

Don José de Shapiro can perhaps settle down here after all, I thought, as I walked back from the bullfight to my hotel. His sons will go to school as Spaniards and parade at night during the café hour, bantering with the dark-eyed girls in the streets. Spain has rejoined Europe. What happened before was an accident of history. No nation—especially a Roman nation—can arrest itself, languishing forever in the sixteenth century.

No nation—except, of course, Spain. What proof had one anyhow that the centuries improved as they went on? The Spaniards knew better. They had seen their empire come and go, one stage ahead of the British. Were they really coming back into Europe now, or would they prefer to go on living by their private formula, in which fanaticism was the obverse of scepticism, and cruelty the strange bedfellow of gentleness?

I thought of the Inquisition. Everything else had happened

before and elsewhere. But the Inquisition was different. For the Jews—as for the other Europeans—it was a ritual of cruelty, an affront to man's humanity. For the Spaniards it was a triumph of consistency.

The Spaniards could treat with the rest of the world as long as it remained outside. But within the Spanish body itself, some constant *auto da fé*—an act of faith with its pyre of victims—had to testify to belief. This was how they waged their civil war, the eternal civil war that they had fought and re-fought for centuries. No mercy was ever asked for or given. Faith demanded its demonstration. With faith appeased, one could be quiet, courteous, gentle.

Back at the hotel, I opened my *Bible in Spain* to the scene at Cordova where the old Carlist priest, no longer permitted to preach in the 'liberal' era of 1835, contents himself and entertains Borrow by recalling the glories of the Inquisition in which he had served as a young man. Here were the Jews again, as large as life—larger indeed.

'Were you troubled with Judaism in these parts?' Borrow asks him.

'Wooh!' he replies. 'Nothing gave so much trouble to the Santa Casa as this same Judaism. Its shoots and ramifications are numerous, not only in these parts but in all Spain; and it is singular enough that even among the priesthood, instances of Judaism of both kinds were continually coming to our knowledge, which it was, of course, our duty to punish.'

'Is there more than one species of Judaism?' asks Borrow.

'I have always arranged Judaism under two heads,' says the old man, 'the black and the white. By the black, I mean the observance of the law of Moses in preference to the precepts of the church; then there is the white Judaism, which includes all kinds of heresies, such as Lutheranism, freemasonry, and the like.'

Borrow expresses his amazement that Judaism should be found among Catholic priests.

'Plenty of it,' says the old man, 'whether of the black or white species. I remember once searching the house of an ecclesiastic who was accused of the black Judaism, and after much investigation we discovered beneath the floor a wooden chest, in which was a small shrine of silver, enclosing three books in black hogskin, which, on being opened, were found to be books of Jewish devotion, written in the Hebrew characters, and of great antiquity. And on being questioned, the culprit made no secret of his guilt but rather gloried in it, saying that there was no God but one, and denouncing the adoration of Maria Santissima as rank idolatry.'

'And between ourselves,' says Borrow, 'what is your opinion of the adoration of this same Maria Santissima?'

'What is my opinion? *Que se io!*' says the old man, shrugging his shoulders. 'But I will tell you. I think, on consideration, that it is quite right and proper. Why not? Let anyone pay a visit to my church, and look at her as she stands there, *tan bonita, tan guapita*—so well-dressed and so genteel—with such pretty flowers, such red and white, and he would scarcely ask me why Maria Santissima should not be adored.'

★ ★ ★

The lecture next morning was a long penetrating study by a German professor, putting the philosophy of Maimonides into its period. I found myself sitting next to a quiet little man who had come, he told me, from Marrakesh. He was with two others from the same town, and he pointed them out to me. There were other visitors also from Morocco, he said, from Safi, Casablanca, and Rabat. Looking at them in the hall, I saw something in their faces that separated them from the other visitors, and as I talked with them, I began to understand what it was. The Jews in these Moroccan towns had lived there without a break for centuries—since the days of Maimonides—long before, indeed: as far back as the days of the Temple, some said. They were in effect Arabs, living in the squalor and ignorance of the *mellah*—the old Jewish quarter—cut off from the Western world, and existing only by fierce devotion to their religion. At the heart of this ancestral faith were two human figures, Moses and

Maimonides, as real to them as Maria Santissima had been to the old priest. Moses was an Arab like themselves, a man close to the desert, a primitive man whose Commandments were all a man needed to know. Maimonides, who had come to live with them for a while at Fez when he fled with his father from the persecutions of Moorish Spain, was not a philosopher with views, but a wise man, the father, the healer, the saint. To the Jewish masses of the *mellah* the word had come that Maimonides was to be honoured. In each town a few who could travel—traders whose work took them outside the narrow streets in which they had been born—banded themselves together to make the pilgrimage to the Cordova celebration. They listened to the lectures with the utmost intensity. They could hardly have understood the philosophy, but their lives were now graced forever by an intimate unity with their teacher.

There was a great serenity in such acceptance. I sat with my new friends all morning. In the afternoon I went with three of them to look at the old mosque, and then we walked for a while along the river bank while they talked to me in French about the lives they led. In the evening we sought out the 'Synagogue of Maimonides' and heard the evening prayers read. It was a building that had been erected far later than Maimonides' time, perhaps two hundred years later. But that made no difference. With its graceful arches and carvings, it seemed to belong to an eternal golden age. Somehow or other it had survived.

So the weeks passed. During the mornings we wandered over the medieval world with Averroes and Duns Scotus, or were led into the intimacies of the *Responsa*, the replies that Maimonides sent to inquirers in many countries on detailed problems of law and life. In the evenings we would gather at a café and tell each other stories, Don José excelling. In the newspapers, we read of a strike in Barcelona, a demonstration in Madrid calling for the return of Gibraltar to the Spanish, a speech of Hitler denouncing the Jews. It was time to go.

★ ★ ★

THE WORDS AND THE MUSIC

I travelled to Gibraltar on Friday in the same bus as the Moroccans, and left them at the bus station with warm farewells. Depositing my bag, I set out to find Dickie Fothergill. He was out when I telephoned the naval station. I left a message and went for a walk. Gibraltar was a cheerful place, yet I looked around me with unbelieving eyes: the sailors, the brick buildings, the tea-shops, the cricket field—it had all overtaken me too quickly.

I strolled down to the harbour, and there on the quay, near the ferry for Tangier, were my Moroccan friends. They greeted me with an outburst of warmth as if we had met in the desert, waving their arms, and chattering away in French.

As I stood with them, there was a great roaring of a car, and a big open Alvis drove up with Dickie at the wheel. 'I thought it was you,' he shouted. 'Just going for a swim. Hop in!'

It was rather strange. Seeing this big blond Englishman waving so cheerfully made it easier for me to realize what I wanted to do. I walked across towards the car. 'I've changed my plans a bit,' I said to him. 'I've decided to go over with my friends here. Following the trail to North Africa.'

He looked across at them. 'Were they at Cordova with you?'

I nodded. 'They're from Marrakesh and Rabat and a few other places. I want to see what it looks like.'

He looked at them and at me and was silent for a moment. 'Well, don't stay away too long, old boy,' he said finally, bending forward to put the car into gear. He paused for a second and looked up. 'You *are* coming back this way?'

'Oh yes, I'll be back.'

With a wave of his hand and a roar from the exhaust he was off down the street. When I rejoined the Moroccans they looked at me questioningly. 'I've decided to come with you,' I told them. 'I'll spend the Sabbath in Tangier.' I went to get my bag, bought a ticket, and sat with them as we crossed the Straits.

I took a room in a small cheap hotel, and went straight to bed. I was very tired. In the morning, I got up early and found my way up into the old quarter. This was no Moorish town as Marrakesh and the others would be, but even here the fetid smell, the crumbling houses, the dark alleys of another world soon enfolded one. Children ran about, with sores dripping from their eyes, and a few scraggy dogs poked for food in piles of rubbish that lay around.

From a small open doorway I heard a low murmur of voices, a vaguely familiar sound, and I walked in. It was a dark low room, with a small dais in the middle from which a man was reading the Law in Hebrew. There were fifteen or twenty men in the room, all wearing prayer shawls. They sat or walked around, some talking, others listening abstractedly. There were some small boys there too. I sat down and listened. The Law was being chanted to a tune I had never heard before, but I knew the words.

Yes, I knew every word. I had heard them first in our little seaport town in the north of England, and I would always hear them that way, with the brisk east wind of the North Sea rattling the windows of the synagogue, and my father walking home with me afterwards, our coats buttoned up tight, to the heavy Sabbath meal. This is how I would hear them. My children, if I had any, would hear something different.

Where were my roots? I looked around wonderingly at the hot dusty streets as I strolled down afterwards towards my hotel. Some part of me, long unrealized, was vivid now. The words of the Law had fallen happily, comfortingly, on my ears. But the chant was different here. Behind the ancient sound, I was listening for cheerful Tyneside voices and the gulls' raucous cry on a cold seashore.

II

JERUSALEM

The year after Spain, I went to Jerusalem. All in all it was a pretty decisive year. Things were never the same, either for Jerusalem or me. In fantasy I can tell myself that it was a year in which I was looking for something like the Dead Sea Scrolls without knowing it, and in any case ten years too soon. Another way is to remember it as the year in which I met Yael.

This was not her name, and saying it makes me realize how quickly the word Jerusalem unlocks the imagination. Everything around Jerusalem is a dream for me, and it seems more truthful to write of it this way. It's certainly more fun.

I could start with Yael—such a pretty Hebrew name if one pronounces it properly: *Ya-ël*, though rather ominous if one thinks of the Book of Judges. But Yael is really the end and not the beginning. In the beginning was a man who had spent quite a few years behind a nice protective hedge. One day he looked up and the hedge was gone. Quite disconcerting.

But at the beginning of that year all seemed in good order. Life had settled down very happily for me between Oxford and London. During the week I had my lectureship in Biblical studies at Oxford to keep me busy. It had now become a Fellowship with which I had started to write a book. For most weekends, and quite a few weekday nights, I was in London, having a delightful time with an amusing, carefree girl who had a job at the Board of Trade and in her own way as a Christian was as keen on Jewish studies as *I* was. What more could a man want?

But there *was* more. The Fellowship encouraged me to travel while writing, and I was off to Palestine. The book I had started was on the 'Midrash'—the Biblical commentaries of the early rabbis. I had been brought up on them, as I had on the vision of 'next year in Jerusalem'. To pursue all these studies in Palestine itself—and by the bounty of Oxford—seemed quite perfect. I was sure that the pilgrimage to Palestine would bring rewards in understanding the subject that I could not even envisage. I talked about it endlessly to Heather, as we walked back from concerts or the theatre to her little flat in Westminster. She was enthusiastic.

I think I liked her enthusiasm more than anything. It was one more proof to me that the two sides of my life had finally found a harmony. In my youth I had been pulled in opposite directions by my intensely orthodox Jewish upbringing and the non-Jewish world around me; but now I had stumbled into a way of living that seemed to bring everything together, and with a sense of constant discovery. There was infinite room in my Hebrew studies for all that I felt about my Jewish past. Everything I read fitted in and added colour and variety—rabbinical legends, classical history, Freud, archaeology—it was like peeling an endless onion, with sharp recognition bringing tears of excitement to one's eyes. And on the other side was Oxford—and Heather. To be reading my father's copy of the Talmud in that ancient, pinnacled background, followed by dinner at High Table and port in the Senior Common Room was some sort of special benediction. As for Heather, with her long fair hair and slender casualness, she seemed to blow away for me so many old ghosts and taboos. When I was in London with her we went to performances of the St Matthew Passion or the Crazy Gang, with perhaps an oyster supper afterwards in De Hemms Bar. She knew half the Shakespeare sonnets by heart and would quote them to me while I stroked her fair hair, lying at peace on the narrow divan in her flat in Westminster.

Westminster! Wasn't that a triumph all by itself? Heather used to say casually that it was so convenient for Whitehall and her job, but I am sure she had really chosen to live there to be in the aura of the Abbey. She was a devout Anglican—rather High. Her first lover had been a curate. As she described him, he was tall and bony, with sandy hair and a straight classical nose. She was always very flippant when she talked of him, but her eyes, I noticed, had a dreamy look. However that was all over now, and there she was, waiting for me at the other end of a telephone —with an Abbey number—languid and passionate. I have always admired the way in which some devout Christians seem to live

JERUSALEM

so easily on both sides of the narrow line between good fun and original sin. The Jews, alas, don't believe in original sin—only in sin. It's a great handicap. But Heather was very adroit at all this. I was very happy with her.

My book on the Midrash, far from being a remote kind of subject, seemed to bridge another of the gaps. As soon as I had explained that it had to do with Biblical readings and exegesis in the early synagogues, her whole theological being rose in my support. The chanting of the Pentateuch, the reading of the Lesson in church—it was all one subject. Everyone took it for granted now, but in fact the origin of it all was rather mysterious. There were plenty of descriptions in the Bible of what had *preceded* the early synagogues—the grim animal sacrifices in the Temple—the pouring of the blood on the altar—the ritual of the High Priest and his assistants; and in the Talmud it had all been elaborated, long after the Temple had been destroyed, into elaborate nostalgic Tractates of rabbinic punctilia about Temple regulations. Yet side by side with this the same rabbis had inherited and developed a tradition of quiet reflection and discussion about man as an individual which was as natural to our present life as the Temple ritual was remote from it. The synagogue was the key—prayers and Bible readings—words instead of blood. The origin of it all seemed worth studying.

I was telling Heather about this—and especially about the Bible readings—one day when we were walking back through St James's Park to her flat, after a choral evensong at St Margaret's. 'I know,' she said. 'There's something about the reading of the Lesson, isn't there? Especially the *First* Lesson, from the Old Testament. It's so—what is it?—so bizarre. There we were today in the middle of the twentieth century listening to Ezekiel prophesying that the Brook Kidron would swarm with a great multitude of fish—it's crazy, isn't it, when you come to think of it? But I just adore it, don't you? I suppose it's because it's gone on for so long. And I love that peculiar moment when he says: "*Here endeth the First Lesson*"—you know: he closes the Bible, and there's a kind of quiet rustle—then someone coughs—and then you hear his feet echoing as he walks back on the stone

87

floor. . . . It's really what I remember best from childhood. It's so *wan*, isn't it? Was it like that in synagogue when you were a child?'

'No, my love, it was not,' I said. 'The thing that I remember best about the Bible reading when I was a small child was my feeling of absolute terror that my father might drop the Scroll of the Law. The Scroll is so holy that I was certain that if my father dropped it there would be a tremendous explosion and the ground would open and swallow us all up—like the story of Korach in the Bible. But he never dropped it. You know it might have been better if he had. . . .'

I could easily recapture that awe in synagogue as a tiny child. My father was the Cantor, and I sat behind him on the dais in a white sailor suit while he lifted up the Scroll, unwrapped it, and then chanted the weekly portion of the Pentateuch to the ancient tune. As I grew older my fears were submerged, and a new interest arose: which members of the congregation would be 'called up' to stand by my father while he chanted? There were priorities here of great social importance to our little community in the north of England. Later I learnt to chant it myself and consequently knew by heart, from countless rehearsals and recitals, every detail of the Pentateuch—first the patriarchs, and then the forty years' wandering the wilderness. Going through the whole Pentateuch once a year, starting in September, I associated the stories in each weekly portion with its own special season—the bare trees and cold emptiness of a northern autumn for the story of the Creation, the bursting spring as we fled from Egypt and crossed the Red Sea, the high summer—with thunder in the air—as Moses let fly with the terrifying curses of Deuteronomy. Each week as we read, the parchment Scroll grew heavier on one side, lighter on the other, until at the great Feast of the Rejoicing of the Law, when the Scroll came to an end, we quickly re-rolled it, ready to start again.

It had all seemed immemorial and unchanging until one day I bumped into German scholarship. Once one has seen German scholarship at work, life is never simple again.

In my case the German scholar was an Austrian called Adolf

JERUSALEM

Buechler, famous for the fantastic patience with which he could pore over written texts and come out with the most original theories. I had taken it for granted, for example, that the custom of reading through the Pentateuch once a year went straight back to the first synagogues. It seemed so natural. But Beuchler, starting with a statement by the Babylonian rabbis that the 'Jews of the West'—that is, of Palestine—went through the Torah in *three* years instead of one, had set out to show from a minute examination of midrashic homilies how you could actually break down the Torah into weekly readings on a triennial cycle. In his view these homilies were always based on the first verse of the weekly reading. By getting the main homilies in order, as collected in different rabbinic books, you could establish the weekly Lessons. Then, from internal evidence, you might be able to establish how *early* the break-up into regular weekly Lessons had become accepted.

'You mean that you might have to set out to look for 156 weekly sermons,' Heather said when I explained the idea.

'Something like that,' I said.

'But is that so terrible?' she asked. 'It sounds rather fun, picking them out.'

'Oh God,' I groaned, 'if it were only as simple as that. You can't just look at the existing text and take it apart. You have to find out if some later editor has put bits in or taken bits out. You have to compare it with other parts of the rabbinic literature in the Talmud. The fact is it's bloody difficult. Not only haven't I got Buechler's scholarship: I haven't got his patience. But I have another idea—much more exciting....'

And then I told her what I would like to do: to find something real in Palestine that would prove the whole thing: to look there for some direct evidence on the Midrash or on the synagogue—some manuscript or other that might lie waiting there, buried in the soil to show directly how synagogue affairs in those days had actually been carried out.

We had just been reading in the *Daily Telegraph* the articles by Dr Torczyner of the Hebrew University of Jerusalem about the discovery and deciphering of the Lachish Letters at Tell Duweir.

Until then no one had ever uncovered any inscription in Hebrew describing contemporary events in the Bible in any detail, and here suddenly were these fabulous glazed potsherds going back to the days of King Jehoiakim, describing Nebuchadnezzar's first attack on the Kingdom of Judah in 598 B.C. We were full of the marvel of this, and I was ready for a similar miracle on my own subject. Suppose, I said to Heather, I found in Palestine some Scroll of the Law actually used in syangogue readings in the early centuries. It wouldn't have to be a whole scroll of the Pentateuch: a section would do, provided it indicated in some way the division into weekly readings. Or it might be a commentary—an introductory verse with a homily following.

'The way Jesus preached in the synagogue at Nazareth?' she asked.

'Something like that,' I said, 'but in its background. All that the New Testament says is that when Jesus went into the synagogue, he was handed the Book of Isaiah, opened it at the verse *The Spirit of the Lord is upon me* and then, when he'd read the passage, began to expound it. What I'd like to know is: was this passage the set reading for the day from the Prophets? Did it correspond to a set passage from the Pentateuch, as the prophetical readings in synagogue do now? Wouldn't it be wonderful to find a scroll that went back as far as this and showed exactly what went on in the synagogue, and how it developed as a place for thought and argument. . . .'

'Why are you always emphasizing the synagogue as a place for argument?' Heather asked. 'Wasn't it a place for prayer?'

'Of course it was,' I said, 'but there was something else about it that seems to me more important, especially as it grew in the early centuries. They didn't just pray: they asked questions, endless questions.'

'You put reason above everything, don't you?'

'Do I? I suppose I do in a way. . . .'

I wasn't quite sure what I was groping for, and why the synagogue was so important to it. Perhaps it was enough for the Jews to have created the synagogue as a place of prayer. But to

JERUSALEM

me their real originality lay in having gone on in their assemblies to superimpose on the prayers a joyful celebration of man as a reasoning being. The Jews had little talent for metaphysics. In their view, truth only existed when one pursued it: and in pursuit of the truth they took off in the Talmud and Midrash on a great splurge of exegesis, history, law, science, anecdote and common sense—a burst of reason and argument that was boundless. It was as if they believed that the free exercise of reason was man's way of saying thank you to God. Maybe they had overdone it a bit over the ages, but on the whole the aim, in human terms, was a noble one and had a certain amount to its credit.

Floating vaguely over my head, I suppose, were all those heroic figures who had somehow emerged out of the synagogue even if they had abandoned it—or never really known it—Spinoza, Marx, Freud, Einstein and all the others. If there was some magic in the synagogue it lay a long way back: perhaps I would feel it when I got to Palestine and saw for myself how it had all started. Of course it was a little far-fetched to hope that I would find actual manuscripts myself. I had no training as an archaeologist and only a mediocre knowledge of the languages and scripts that might be involved. But things were being discovered. There were the Lachish Letters; and there had been the Ras Shamra inscriptions in Syria some years earlier. There were lots of smaller discoveries all the time. Something had started—something new, for until now the soil and rock of Palestine had not yielded up any of its real secrets. Perhaps the difference now was the presence in Palestine of the new settlements of Jews and their living identification with the ancient language. It seemed to give the work of the Jewish archaeologists a fresh kind of insight, as if in preparation for great discoveries. I was probably hoping, even as an amateur, that some of this new learning might rub off on me.

★ ★ ★

This was the Palestine of the British Mandate. Admittedly if one went there as a Jew it was to see the miracle of the Jews rebuilding their ancient land—the kibbutzim, the orange groves, and all that; but going from England had at the same time a slight flavour of visiting Bermuda or Kenya. The British were in charge, dispensing their famous mixture of superiority and fair play. Yet there was a difference even from the British side. The British were in charge here in a highly personal and meaningful way—just as they had been in charge of the Bible since 1611 because of the Authorized Version.

Now that Palestine has become Israel and Jordan it is not easy to recapture the unique brand of parental responsibility (spelling both love and reproof) which characterized the British attitude in those days to Palestine and the Jews who had settled there. For most of the British, brought up sturdily on the Old Testament, Palestine was much more instinctively the land of Abraham, Isaac and Jacob than of Jesus. And in assuming the Mandate in 1917 to help establish the Jewish National Home, they had not started from scratch, even in a technical sense. For eighty years or more, since the spacious days of Palmerston and the good Consul Finn, the British Consulate in Jerusalem had voluntarily extended the protection of the British Government to some of the Jews in Palestine, and not merely to keep a foot in the Turkish door. In the mind of an Englishman it all went back somehow to schoolboy tales of Richard the Lion Heart and the Crusades. For those titillated by culture, there was the Palestine Exploration Fund, select and well-dressed gatherings in Hinde Street to hear lectures by Petrie and Robinson. At a more popular level, there were archaeological drawings in the *Illustrated London News*. And for everybody there was the memory of Old Testament tales at Sunday School. The British *liked* to be in charge of Palestine. They meant to do well there, if only the Jewish settlers would be reasonable and let things go along at a steady British pace. One would never, of course, feel the same kind of admiration for the Jews that one felt for the Arabs—and most particularly for the Arabs of the desert. The desert was, after all, the British version of the Wild West, and the Arab on his white steed a combination of cowboy and medieval knight.

JERUSALEM

But the Jews, if they behaved, had a place there too, and indeed a very special place, all their own.

Heather lent me a splendid book when I told her I was going: *Early Travels in Palestine*, published in 1848 by Henry G. Bohn, of York Street, Covent Garden, under the learned editorship of one Thomas Wright, Esq., Fellow of the Society of Antiquaries. It was a compilation, in the delightful type and binding of the time, of nine or ten narratives of pilgrimages to the Holy Land, undertaken from A.D. 700 onwards, largely from England. It had been given to her as a Christmas present two years earlier by her curate, 'the Hon. George' as she always called him playfully; and it was, incidentally, one of the few visible relics of the curate that I saw in her flat. Heather was inclined to be rather mysterious about the curate. He was, it seemed, a genuine Hon. and they had been lovers when she was a history student at Oxford. Why had he taken flight? Had the Lord (his father) disapproved? Or perhaps his Bishop? Nothing explicit was said. Some of the clues dropped were in his favour, others left the smell of a prig in the air. This book was one of the good things: a well-chosen Christmas present. Heather had adored it, even if, as I saw, some of the pages were still uncut. Her favourite, she told me, was the long leisurely account by Sir John Maundeville of the pilgrimage he had made in 1322; but she had dipped into others too. She was very fond—as of course she would be—of the journey by the Anglo-Saxon Willibald, who had set off from Hampshire in A.D. 718. All very British, it seemed, until I spotted, pages uncut, a pilgrimage I already knew about—*The Travels of Rabbi Benjamin of Tudela*, who had set out on *his* journey from Saragossa in 1164.

I think that the worthy Mr Wright made a mistake to call him *Rabbi* Benjamin. His name in Hebrew is *R. Benjamin*, the R standing for *Rab* or *Reb*, which means *Mr*—or perhaps we should say in his case, as he came from Spain, *Señor*. I had read his story before, in Hebrew; but it was rather different to see him here, boxed-in by characters like Sigurd the Crusader and Bertrandon de la Brocquiere. The Christian pilgrimages in this book are so beautifully pious and ancient: R. Benjamin, by contrast, is so painfully practical and parochial. Wherever he goes—on his three-year journey, the main thing he has on his mind is to list the number of Jews in each place, the names of the leading citizens, and how they all earn their living. He is thrilled with Italy. Lucca is 'a large city which contains about forty Jews, the principal of whom are R. David, R. Samuel, and R. Jacob'. A journey of six days brings him to Rome, 'where two hundred Jews live who are very much respected and pay tribute to no one'. When, after the three years of wandering, he finally reaches Jerusalem, he achieves what must be the dizziest anticlimax in literature. To the Psalmist, Jerusalem was 'the city which men called the perfection of beauty'. But R. Benjamin has other things on his mind. Jerusalem has a numerous population, he says, and then continues: 'The dyeing-house is rented by the year, and the exclusive privilege of dyeing is purchased from the king by the Jews of Jerusalem.'

I am, of course, being terribly unfair to Señor Benjamin. His story is, in fact, packed with a great deal of information. The generous Mr Wright says in his Introduction that Benjamin, 'who was evidently a merchant, describes what he saw with more good sense and accuracy than the Christian travellers of the same age.' Trust an Englishman to be fair. The truth is that it depends on what one is looking for. Just a page or two earlier in Mr Wright's Introduction there is a brief account of a pilgrimage undertaken in A.D. 868 by 'a noble Breton, of the name of Frotmond.' For some reason, it made a special appeal to me:

'Frotmond, who, with his brother, had committeed one of those deeds of blood which so often stain the history of the Middle Ages, was condemned by the church to a penance, not uncommon in those times. A chain was close riveted round his body and his arms; and in this condition, covered only with a coarse garment, his head sprinkled with ashes, he was to visit, barefoot, the holy places, and wander about until God should deign to relieve him of his burthen. In the fourth year of his wanderings he returned to France, and went to the monastery of Redon, where he was miraculously delivered from his chains, which had already eaten deep into his flesh, at the tomb of St Marcellinus. . . .'

How far this all is from R. Benjamin. One thinks of Benjamin more readily as he would be today, travelling by El-Al Airline, with a Diners' Club card in his wallet. And Frotmond? Ah yes, we know Frotmond well enough too: the central character in all Graham Greene's novels.

★ ★ ★

I was getting into the mood for the journey; packing books, working on my Arabic, sorting out my ideas about the book I was writing. I had decided to concentrate for the moment on one part of the Midrash—the commentary on the Book of Lamentations, since this Midrash was particularly rich in historical material about Jerusalem at the time of the Romans. But I also had a private reason. This was a Midrash I had read with my father, and there was a character in it that I wanted to catch up with.

Superficially the Midrash on *Lamentations* is quite an easy book to read, full of horror stories about the cruelties of the Romans during the different Jewish revolts. All the Roman generals and Emperors are villains, but the arch-villain is Hadrian, the Emperor who crushed the last revolt—by Bar Cochba in A.D. 135—and thus finally deprived us of our homeland. All the grimmest stories are pinned on him; and the rabbis couldn't even mention his name without adding a curse: '*Hadrian, may his bones be crushed. . . .*'

He was a larger-than-life monster to me in my childhood, much worse even than Haman in the Book of Esther, since we had finally got the better of Haman and turned him into a clown. But Hadrian had stayed monstrous to the end. The essence of fear is mystery. It might have made quite a difference to me as a child if I had known that that far-off shadowy figure—the scourge of the Jews—had in fact set out to crush Bar Cochba's revolt from the very area in the north of England where we lived. The ruins of Hadrian's Wall—mighty and ancient—were only twenty miles away, though to my father and me it was all as unknown as the Great Wall of China. It could never have occurred to me that a monster in my father's Hebrew books could have had an English existence at nearby Hexham, building his great barrier across the neck of England to keep out those craggy Picts and Scots, the ancestors of my friends Jim Macgregor and Alistair Macleod. To have brought Hadrian down to earth like this would have meant recognizing that his war with the Jews was just a short incident in a busy life, whereas to my father and me and all of us the destruction of the Temple and the scattering of the Jews was the central fact around which all history and all existence turned.

'*Next Year in Jerusalem!*' How cold life would have been without this great sigh of comfort and hope at the end of the long Passover Seder Service. Perhaps even more than this, how I would have missed that most satisfying wake which we indulged in every year at the Fast of Ab—the anniversary of both Destructions—when the whole of our little congregation sat in mourning on low stools, the very pious having sprinkled ashes on their hair (like Frotmond), while my father rocked back and forth chanting the sad strophes of *Lamentations* to some ancient tune in a minor key—a dirge of unutterable beauty and grief. The Fast of Ab comes in high summer, usually in July; and on the next day I would be out playing cricket on the sands or on some green English field, with sing-song Tyneside voices shouting: 'Come on, *run*, you duffer!', or if I was lucky: 'Oh, jolly good catch!' I lived happily, it seemed, on both sides of an iron curtain. The Jewish world was one place, England another. There was never any real indication to me that they might be one until many years later my headmaster, Sedgewick, gave me a book—a fat 700-page book with red linen covers and gold letters on its comfortable spine. Plunging into it that first night had been more exciting to me than Chapman's Homer.

I was packing it now, old and worn as it was, to take with me: *The Historical Geography of the Holy Land.* I had only to hold it in my hand again to recapture the feeling of that first reading. Palestine had been until then a place in the Bible, with every town and village as familiar as Barsetshire and as unreal. And suddenly I was seeing it through the mind of a man who had been in every one of these villages himself, could name every type of rock or tree, had explored every journey, re-fought every battle, listened to every prophecy, read every chronicle, and then brought it all together slowly and reflectively as if saying that if the Bible meant anything at all it was worth thinking about slowly, not with *part* of one's mind—the part reserved for church or synagogue—but with all that had ever passed through it, every scrap of knowledge or experience. It was the Midrash of a Victorian geographer, written precisely for me fourteen years before I was born.

The author had enjoyed the mellifluous name of The Very Rev. Sir George Adam Smith. As a young man he had wandered over Palestine on foot and horseback, year after year, looking at the rocks and caves, talking to the Arabs, marvelling at the relation of the land itself to the sound of Hebrew, talking in the same breath of the Hittites and the Amorites, the Greeks and the Crusaders—and then, to give it absolute reality for him, bringing it all back to his native Scotland. This was the quality which turned it from a textbook into poetry. Palestine was a more magic Scotland: the glens and moors plus Revelation—absurd but entrancing.

I could hardly pack the book now without at least dipping into it, and I opened it happily to a favourite chapter on the *Shephelah*—the low hills of chalk and limestone that rise from the Philistine plain. There it was—*a rough, happy land, with its glens and moors, its mingled brushwood and barley-fields.* He saw this craggy land—and one understands why a Scotsman would—as a font of character—*just the home for strong border-men like Samson*; and he goes on to describe the constant guerrilla warfare it produced—David against the Philistines, the Maccabees against the Syrians, Richard the Lion Heart against Saladin. . . .

I had to smile, reading it now. I had forgotten how slow it was, how ponderous, how Victorian. And suddenly, turning the pages, I smiled more broadly to re-discover an intimate acquaintance—a hero to him, a monster to me. He is writing, in his wonderful Victorian way, of Beit-Jibrin, a ruined Arab village that had once been a busy converging point for a number of old Roman roads—

MEMOIRS OF A SPECIAL CASE

Many times, as our horses' hoofs strike pavement on the Roman roads of Palestine and we lift our eyes to the unmistakable line across the landscape, we pilgrims from the far north are reminded that these straight lines cross our own island, and we are thrilled with some imagination of what the Roman Empire was and how it grasped the world. But by Beit-Jibrin this feeling grows still more intense, for the Roman buildings there are mostly the work of the same emperor who built the wall on the Tyne, and hewed his way through Scotland to the shores of the Pentland Firth. . . .

Good old Hadrian, may his bones be crushed. Everything hung together if one looked long enough. With enough patience. I might even have found here, in his passages on caves, the vital link to my own project. But my mind was probably too cluttered. It needed an intuition that I lacked. It was in fact Heather who, when I showed her this chapter on the night I was leaving, went on to ask about the caves.

We had been talking about *Passage to India*, and perhaps it was this which had riveted her mind on caves and what can happen in them. There was a brief passage in this chapter which remarked how *the soft chalk of the district lent itself admirably to the hewing of intricate caves*, and Heather said casually:

'Of course the Bible's full of cave-stories, isn't it? The cave of Adullam. . . .'

'The cave of Machpelah,' I prompted.

'David and Saul in the cave of En-Gedi. . . .'

'Wasn't that a dirty trick by David. . . .'

'You mean pinching Saul's cloak when Saul went in *to cover his feet*, as they say? Mean as hell. But the place must be honeycombed with caves. Oh God, wouldn't it be marvellous to go on a hike, with rucksacks, sleeping in caves. . . .'

'Sheltering from the early rain and the latter rain, no doubt,' I suggested.

'No, but seriously,' she said. 'One could plan to follow some historic route—like the Pilgrim's Way to Canterbury. I wanted to do that once with the Honourable George, but we didn't manage it. It would be much more marvellous in Palestine. Say follow the wanderings of Abraham, or John the Baptist. Oh no, that's the Wilderness: too grim. Up on the coast at Acre would be better—say looking at Crusader Castles. . . .' She broke off. 'They're surely not all *chalk* caves?'

'Oh no,' I said. 'He's always writing about the limestone hills —all the mountains of Judaea down to the Dead Sea, and on the other side too. . . .'

'Where you get all those old natural caves—secret caves. God, you might go into one to cover your feet, and there, sealed up inside for countless centuries. . . .'

'Is an old Crusader in his coat of mail. . . .'

'Yes, or something older still—some old manuscripts. . . .'

I laughed. 'The Bible, you mean? With the three-year readings clearly marked? Oh, come on. . . .'

She laughed too. 'Yes, I know. But I'd love you to find something about your old Midrash. Make you so happy, wouldn't it?' She broke off. 'Oh dear, I shall miss you terribly.'

I put my arm round her as we stood near her window, with its little glimpses of the Westminster buildings and St James's Park. 'I'll miss you too,' I said. We heard the chime of bells from a church, and then, a little later, the sound of a bugle call from the Wellington Barracks. O *que le son du cor*. . . .

'We should be listening to that together on the rampart of some old Crusader Castle,' she said. 'Oh golly, I wish I were going with you.'

'I wish you were too,' I said, stroking her hair.

She turned and wound her arms around me, resting her cheek on mine. 'Oh darling,' she murmured. 'Of course you don't. You're miles and miles away already. But I don't mind. I do understand.'

In the corner of her little room were my suitcases, all newly labelled. She could see the same labels invisibly on me. I began to say something, but she stopped me with a soft kiss.

★ ★ ★

A slow boat to Suez, and a slow overnight train from there to Jerusalem. It was not quite R. Benjamin's three years, but enough of a pause to let the normal world slip quietly away, with so much that I thought I was carrying with me.

I was laden with introductions, but there was nobody I wanted to see—nobody, that is, to whom I needed an introduction. For the first time in my life, it seemed to me, I was completely happy alone, wandering with equal freedom through the narrow alleys of the Old City or along the open streets of the town outside, stopping for an orange juice or a coffee from time to time, talking to passers-by—merchants, pedlars, beggars, students—but always aware of the tremulous light and the endless variety of colour, smell and sound—the great mounds of fruit and vegetables in the markets, the tireless rattle of a thousand hammers working on metal, the strange sour-sweet smells of oil and incense, the bloody carcasses of meat besieged by a million flies, the whine of saws and the woody perfume of shavings, the ceaseless ring of hammer on stone where shirtless men, glowing fresh from the sun, sat squaring off the blocks for the new houses rising everywhere. The shrill Old City sound of high-pitched argument in a hundred tongues was as desperate and murderous as the clamour of a jungle, and at the same time as free and innocent as the piping of great flocks of birds. And in the looks which met one—narrow, desperate eyes, soft brown eyes, laughing eyes, sad far-away eyes—one saw them all at once, and in one person—like the dazzling alternation of white light and shade on the pavement; for there was no simplicity here, nothing ordered or accepted, but a constant shifting of mood, a relentless struggle with the enemy, with one's neighbour, with authority—and yet with it an exhilarating love of life, a laughing acceptance that the blows and bounty of Providence were equally part of human existence—the trickery of thieves, the joys of friendship, the stab in the back, the unbreakable bonds of blood. There was no ease in Zion, not until one stood outside the Old City under the ancient Temple rock, or climbed Mount Scopus and looked out across the eternal landscape to the Dead Sea and the blue hills of Moab. Or at night, when, walking along King George Avenue, one met a British policeman and all was for the moment safe.

JERUSALEM

I had started a routine of going up every morning in the bus to the Hebrew University on Mount Scopus to listen to lectures or work in the Library, after which I would wander back on foot, in the middle of the day, across the Vale of Hinnom towards the Old City for a leisurely dreamy walk along the top of the city walls to descend at the Damascus or Jaffa Gate, as the fancy took me. There were rarely any others on the top of the wall at that time of day—only an occasional Arab, with a prowling look in his eye, or an Englishwoman, with a big hat, painting away busily at a watercolour. Up on the wall one had the Psalmist's feeling, that Zion was a city lifted up—*beautiful in elevation, the joy of the whole earth*. Looking out, one saw the cypress-dotted hills rolling away, especially to the west and the deep tortured declivity of the Jordan; and inside, sheltered by the wall, was the warmth of a living community, the high stone walls, the churches, the squares and alleys—the agglomerate huddle of 3,000 years—*Jerusalem is builded as a city that is compact together*. It seemed to matter little that the huge hewn stones of the massive outer wall had been quarried and built up by Suleiman the Magnificent. To see any great hewn stones sent one's mind back immediately to the Temple of that other Solomon, even more perhaps than to the period of really great building, under Herod. It was important to me to understand the layout of the walls because of their relevance to the stories of the Destruction in the Midrash I was studying. What were the fortifications that the Romans had had to breach? Today there was only one wall, but Josephus spoke of three. Relics of the Third Wall had, in fact, been discovered just a few years earlier when some rich Arab of the Nashashibi clan was digging the foundations for a new villa to the north of the Old City. It was ironic when one thought of it. The Third Wall had been built to safeguard the new houses that were mushrooming to the north of the Old City in the boom period of Herod. It had failed to hold off the Roman onslaught, and all Jerusalem had been destroyed. But now, with Palestine reviving under the Jews after 2,000 years of sleep, the suburbs to the north were needed again—by an Arab; and out of the soil came the

Third Wall. If it worked this way, might not one find other things?

It was all so different from dear old Buechler poring over his written texts. Abstract deduction—like all intellectualism—could lead one astray so easily. I thought of this a good deal, and particularly one day when, standing under the site of the old Temple, I recalled Buechler's brilliant but bizarre theory about the ancient Sanhedrin of Jerusalem. It was just above this very spot that the Sanhedrin had always met—*in the hall of hewn stone*. History had given us a clear image of these seventy bearded old men wielding their own authority, rather like the American Supreme Court. But Buechler, out of the deep resources of his mind, had put forward the theory one day in a famous study that all our ideas about the Sanhedrin—and by implication of the trial of Jesus—were wrong. There had not been *one* Sanhedrin, he argued, but two sitting side by side, each with seventy members, one a political body composed of Sadducees, and the other a religious body composed of Pharisees. The religious Sanhedrin—the Pharisees from whom all Jewish rabbinic tradition flowed—had no power at this time to deal with any offence involving capital punishment. They concerned themselves solely with interpreting Temple matters and other questions of religious nicety. It was the other Sanhedrin—upper-class Sadducees anxious only to get rid of trouble-makers and keep in well with the Romans—who dealt with political affairs and could recommend the death sentence. But wasn't it a little odd that no one living at the time had ever referred explicitly to two Sanhedrins? Perhaps it was, said Buechler; but the written references, if properly interpreted, showed that there *must* have been two—and on he went with his argument, exciting intellectually, but in the end just a demonstration on paper. I thought, looking up at the rock with its myriad mysterious colours, of the years of study which Buechler had put into this theory, and how a single document buried in this rock, or somewhere else in Palestine, could prove more than all the theories in the world. Strolling back to my hotel I began to wonder again if Palestine would ever yield some tangible proof for his other speculation, on the triennial cycle of Bible readings. These rocks and stones, this rich earth, still held all the secrets of history, it seemed to me; but I had no idea how to start looking.

* * *

I had been in Palestine for a week, dreaming my way slowly, enjoying the hectic trilingual world of Arabic, Hebrew and English (with German and Yiddish peeping through) but not coming down to earth at any point. So much of the argument around me was political, in the desperate sense. The British Government had just revived the proposal for a Legislative Council representing all elements in Palestine. To the Jews this proposal meant simply that Jewish immigration would be throttled and all economic and agricultural development held back. This was not an issue which could be argued fiercely by the parties concerned followed by friendly drinks afterwards in the local pub. It was an issue—with others like it—of life and death. Only to the British officials could it be part of a daily job to be put away at night—and not even to all of them. As a Jew I sympathized instinctively with the frustration of the Zionists at being held back from the miraculous work they were doing, yet I was reluctant to get into the struggle. In some way I was still floating on a cloud of delight to be there at all; to see around me under the bluest of skies all the places I had known from childhood, to look up at night in wonder at the stars, not faraway pinpoints of light, but a thick cluster of brightness, close enough to touch. I knew at last what Abraham saw when he heard the voice: '*Look now towards Heaven and count the stars: but thou canst not number them. . . .*'

I was staying, in a de-personalized way, in a little hotel off Ben Jehudah Street. I had given the address to Heather before I left, and when I got back there on the day I had been considering the Sanhedrin there was a fat letter from her waiting on the table in my tiny room. For some reason best unknown to myself I didn't read it immediately, but slipped it into my pocket and went down to the Café Vienna for something to eat.

Walking through the door I saw that the tables were all full, except for one where a small, rather round man was sitting. I slumped down, tired after my walk, and pulled out Heather's letter, feeling somehow cross and conscience-stricken. Then I looked up. The little man was grinning broadly. There was nothing to do but smile back; and suddenly, looking at him directly, it seemed to me that his face was familiar.

'*Shalom!*' he said engagingly. 'You are from England, eh?' He indicated the letter with its bold royal stamps. 'We are *landsleit*. I lived there for six months before I came here. Ah—beautiful country—beautiful people—only terrible politicians, eh?'

I was looking hard, wondering where I had met him. But I was already feeling better, and could smile back happily. 'Beautiful when the sun shines,' I said. 'I'm not missing the winter weather. Were you there in the summer?'

'I was there for part of the winter,' he said. 'Cold, wet, frost, fog—and to me it was Heaven. I had just got out of Germany. Ah, you English. You have no idea. The *weather*! What is that? You are *free*! *Live*! Who cares about the weather? Will you have a cup of coffee with me? Now coffee is better *here*: coffee you can't make in England. My name is Shapiro.' He got up and extended his hand across the table.

I told him my name, and accepted the coffee. Shapiro. Something was coming back. A common enough name, but I had known a Shapiro and I looked at him again. Might they be brothers, or did all Shapiros look like this?

'I have been wondering,' I said. 'You look very like a Mr Shapiro I met last spring—in Spain.'

His face lit up. 'You met my brother Yossilë! This is fantastic. Oh, at the celebration—yes?—for Maimonides?'

'Yes, in April.' I was terribly pleased myself to be reminded of that strange fiesta. 'It was wonderful. Jews there from all over the world, and your brother was in the middle of everything....'

'Don't I know my brother?'

'Is he still so happy there, in Madrid?'

Shapiro's face clouded. 'Oh, he left Spain this summer. He decided it can't last. He has gone to settle in the Argentine.'

Then his face brightened a little. 'So you see he is still Don José.'

We laughed. *Don José de Shapiro.* It seemed funny enough when one thought of Yossilë. 'Why didn't he come here?' I asked.

'I advised him not to,' said Shapiro. 'Do you know, things are not too easy here. First it is not easy to come—the Immigration Quota. Your British politics! Less than a thousand this year, and mostly direct from Germany and Poland. And then even when you *are* here. . . .'

'You seem happy enough. . . .'

'I am the older brother. I shall manage. But Yossilë . . . he is the younger one. He should go to a new country.'

'Don't you miss each other?'

'Yes, we do, we do. But who knows? Perhaps if things are good there I might join him, or if things get better here he could join me. And then we do business now. He sends me leather from the Argentine to sell here, and I send him art things— from the Bezalel—which he sells to the Jews in the Argentine. They are very keen Zionists: they buy everything. It is convenient. A Jew must live. And you? You are in business? No, I can see. A lawyer, eh?'

'No, a teacher—and a student. I'm writing a book. . . .'

'A *writer!*' His tone grew most reverent. 'Oh, here there is so much to write about. I will show you. I can arrange. You want to see Palestine. I have tours: one of my men—Dov—will drive you in his car. You must see the kibbutzim, and Haifa, and Safed—and outside—Damascus, Baalbeck, Petra. . . . I shall arrange it all. . . .'

It was impossible to stop him. 'I have no money for all that,' I began.

'Money?' He laughed. 'What is money? You English are too serious. You are here, you are young—you don't have to work out this and that—what you can afford, what you can't afford. You must see everything, do everything. What is money for? If you need money there are ways to earn it. Are you here alone?'

I nodded.

'Not married?'

'No, not married.'

'Not engaged either?'

'Not engaged.'

He sat back, very pleased at something. 'You have time, you have time. A friend of Yossilë's. . . . For you I can do things. Where are you living?'

I told him the hotel. He pulled a face. '*That* hotel! For you? A writer? Oh no, you must have a better place. Yes, yes. . . .' A thought had quickly come to him. 'I know the place: just for you.' He turned and called to a man sitting two or three tables away. 'Mosheh! Come here. A friend of Josef. From Spain.'

'From Spain?' People looked up as the man rose and sidled across—a weedy-looking man with a cavernous face and great hollow eyes. 'So,' he said in a high nasal voice. 'Ein Spanier?'

'You are a fool, Mosheh,' Shapiro told him as the man slid into a seat. 'Does he *look* like a Spaniard? He is an Englishman. I could see immediately. A writer. He needs a place to live. What is with Amram's flat? Has he gone yet?'

'A flat?' I began. . . . Shapiro waved his arm for me to be quiet.

Mosheh was stroking his nose reflectively. 'Amram goes away tomorrow, early in the morning,' he said, 'but his sister Miriam is coming in from Petach Tikvah.'

'Miriam? Why does she have to come in just now? Does she have any reason? Couldn't she come in some other time?'

Mosheh shrugged his shoulders. 'She has to make arrangements for her cousin to come in next month from Roumania.'

'Yes, yes,' Shapiro agreed. 'But for that she doesn't have to have Amram's flat. She could have your room.'

'And me?'

'You can stay with your mother for a few days. Is that so bad? You need some good food anyhow. You are like a skeleton.'

They talked for a few minutes in rapid German and then Mosheh got up to go and make the arrangements. '*Shalom*,' he said to me mournfully, and was off.

'That Mosheh,' Shapiro said. 'He helps me in my business, but he is so stupid. Ah well, now I will tell you. But first we must eat. Have you eaten? No? Why did you just order coffee? Waiter, waiter. . . .'

We ordered some sandwiches and Shapiro sat back. He had taken me over. I was to call him by his first name, Yitzchak (Isaac). The flat was in a converted Arab house—a fine old house turned by the architect Bernstein into four very nice flats, the smallest inhabited by his friend Amram. The cost would be nominal. He would send a young Yemenite girl to clean and cook for me.

And then, as we sat eating our sandwiches and drinking more coffee, he looked at me slyly and said: 'Your letter? You have no wish to read it?'

I took it in my hand and looked at the postmark, clean and definite like everything British: *London, S.W.1. 9.30 p.m.* She had sat writing it in the evening after coming back from the office, with the bells of Westminster chiming the hours, and the sound of the bugle coming in across the Park. Then she had muffled herself up against the cold and fog, and gone downstairs to catch the last post. I put it back into my pocket. 'I will read it later,' I said smiling.

For some reason he was pleased. 'You have all the time in the world,' he said, waving his arm. 'All the time in the world.'

★ ★ ★

There was a telephone message at the hotel from what had sounded like a Mr Biskim. He would telephone again later. I had no idea who Mr Biskim might be, but it all became clear when I read Heather's letter. She had discovered the day after I had left that Nick Briscombe, a cousin of hers in the Colonial Service, had been transferred some time ago to the High Commissioner's staff in Palestine. She was writing to him by the same post to tell him all about me. (*'All about me'*: that sounded a bit ominous.) He was great fun: had been mad about acting at Oxford: played in the O.U.D.S.: was a great practical joker. . . . There was a knock at the door: the hotel-owner to say that Mr Biskim was telephoning again.

His voice at the other end was a nice bellow of welcome. 'Heard all about you from Heather,' he said. 'Isn't she a great girl? We must meet. How long will you be here?'

'A few months, I hope.'

'A few months? Oh, that's great. I say, have you ever done any acting?'

'Acting?' Was this the O.U.D.S. enthusiast, or the practical joker? Perhaps both.

'Yes. I'm organizing a group here. We're putting on a play. Gets everybody together—Arabs and Jews—they're both so difficult, you know. Oh, forgive me, I forgot. But you know what I mean. Were you in the O.U.D.S. at Oxford?'

'I'm afraid not.'

'Oh, it doesn't matter. We can talk about it. I'm really phoning about a party the High Commissioner's giving on Thursday up here, at Government House. I gave them your name. They'll send you a card, but I wanted to be sure you could come. Are you free? Nine on?'

'Well....'

'Oh good. We can meet then. Splendid.'

I put the phone down and went back to Heather's letter. She had had a terrible day at the Board of Trade. Her chief had been unreasonable. She hated the whole thing. But she'd gone back to the flat and had a couple of stiff whiskies and felt better. She'd been reading the new novel by Sinclair Lewis which she'd finally got from the Library after weeks of waiting. Not very good. There was an interesting series of talks on the wireless about the Great Cathedrals of Europe; at least the first one on Chartres had been quite good. She'd bought a new hat to cheer herself up. And she missed me very much.

I missed her too. Life had been very comfortable in that orderly round of Oxford and London. I looked out of the window on to the back door of the hotel where an Arab, pulling at a donkey that was loaded sky-high with baskets carrying enormous marrows and cabbages together with a great assortment of outsize tomatoes and radishes and the usual oranges and grapefruit, was waving his hands violently at the wife of the owner of the hotel, arguing, laughing, protesting. . . . Two tall, curly-bearded Yemenite Jews, in their long striped shirts, were clearing out some rubbish in the courtyard, shouting back good-humouredly to the Arab. Inside the hotel someone was trying to play Chopin on an old cracked piano.

I pulled out my books. I had to force myself to do at least three hours every day of straight Midrash translation and the accompanying notes, or the job would hang over me. I started on some long harrowing stories based on the verse: *For these things I weep*—Jewish girls being shipped to Roman houses of prostitution and throwing themselves into the sea—children being slain in front of their parents—all very disturbing. After a while I shifted to some passages on dream interpretation, all designed to show how clever the rabbi was compared with a certain ignorant Cuthean who was doing dream interpretations in the market-place. The rabbi's interpretations were, in fact, rather startling, the first particularly, where the rabbi said bluntly: 'The significance of that dream is that the man has had intercourse with his mother.' Ahah! This would need quite a footnote. But they grew less interesting, and I decided that I would have to read up some studies of dream interpretation in classical times in order to put it all into its context. I broke off and decided to write Heather a letter. But I sat there with my pen in my hand, wondering what to say. There was nothing of myself that I felt able to give. A postcard would be better. I went out and bought one—of a husky big-breasted Jewish girl holding a great pile of oranges in her arms. As I dropped it in the letter box with the briefest of messages it seemed to fall emptily—a hollow word in a hollow box. This mood was absurd, I felt. I must do something.

It was dark now, and the street was full of cheerful noisy people—lean sunburnt men in blue shirts open at the neck, solid young Jewesses with proud flashing eyes, well-dressed burghers—German refugees, no doubt—scurrying to their Hebrew lessons or lectures on art, Arabs gliding through the streets on missions I could never hope to fathom. I strolled along aimlessly in the dusky perfumed night and suddenly thought what I might do. I could see my new Arab house. Shapiro had told me the name of the street.

It was quite a walk from the centre of the town through a rather deserted area by an Arab cemetery, emerging into a little group of quiet streets with a variety of old-looking houses set out pleasantly around gardens and courtyards. The atmosphere was relaxed here: it would be a good place to work. I turned back, and taking a different route towards the centre of the town found myself after a while in a rather sleazy-looking Arab section, where the men, in their short Western jackets and long Arab skirts, gave me a curious glance as I strolled by. I pushed open the door of a café—a dirty but cheerful-looking place—a couple of tables on the street and a disarray of tables inside, some very bright and some shady lights, with the wireless blaring Arab songs. Two or three groups of Arabs, dressed in Western clothes, sat whispering together, sipping coffee or other drinks. They all looked up when I went in and sat down. I could feel their dark calculating eyes on me. A man—probably the owner—came over and asked in English what I would like. I felt for a moment like reciting some verses from the Koran, which was about all that I could do easily in Arabic: but I asked for coffee. A man with a pile of rugs on his shoulder put his head through the door and began to make his way towards me. But I waved him away. Then a young boy, with brown velvet eyes, came over and sat down, saying nothing—just smiling shyly. There was a burst of laughter from the men at the other tables, a squealing kind of laughter. They called out things to the boy that I could understand quite clearly even if the words were obscure. I saw them rubbing their hands together lasciviously while they joked and shouted. The wireless wailed on with its sharp and exciting Oriental intervals. I sat it out for a while and got up to go, giving the boy the coins from the change. He followed me eagerly outside, accompanied by a new squeal of laughter from the men. I waved him away but he ran along beside me in the dark: 'You want girl, maybe,' he said, trying to pull my arm. 'Come, come.' He tugged away smilingly. 'Pretty girl, young girl, very young.' I stopped for a minute and looked at him. I had to smile too at his friendly earnestness, the tousled hair, the laughing eyes. 'You like boy?' he insisted. 'You like girl? Very young? You like hashish?' Perhaps I did like them, but I could only laugh back at him and give him more coins. He ran after me for a little while, but stopped as I got nearer the town centre. I turned at the corner and waved to him, feeling human again.

* * *

Shapiro was round first thing in the morning with Dov the taxi-driver, a great hulking swarthy Roumanian. I placed him immediately as the strong-arm man in Shapiro's entourage—Mosheh, snivelling and hollow-eyed, for arguing with people like Miriam, Dov for the rough work. In some indefinable way I was beginning to get the feeling that Shapiro was not a man but an operation. However, the muscle-man was friendly enough as he picked up my bags easily, despite their book-laden weight, and put them in his car, a heavy Buick. As we drove round to the flat, Shapiro told me that Amram, whom he had seen the previous night, was delighted at the arrangement. He was off to Haifa *en route* to Paris, for some business they were doing; and later in the year he might be in England. Perhaps I had a flat in London that I could let him use, or knew somebody who had. It didn't really matter, but it was always good to ask, Shapiro said, chattering away ceaselessly. He fell silent as we walked through a little courtyard into the tiled hall of the house, with its high doors opening into what was to be my home, a large room facing the court and a small kitchen off it—a handsome grey marble floor strewn with rugs, high french windows, a beautifully inlaid mosaic around the fireplace, which held a wood stove. It was all cool and utterly delightful. I turned to thank Shapiro and found him smiling peacefully. The Yemenite girl—Ushah—would come in the next day or the day after.

It was nearer to the town centre than I had thought, but I drove back with them as I meant to go up to the University as usual. There was no hurry, however, and Shapiro readily accepted my invitation to have a coffee. He seemed, indeed, to be expecting it as the opportunity to continue our conversation. 'I have been thinking,' he said, as we sat down in the Vienna. 'You spoke of money. The rent here is not much. You can pay me tomorrow or the next day. Amram has left the arrangements to me. I suppose you could do with some money. A writer, I know, doesn't earn much. . . .'

'Nothing at all with my kind of writing,' I said.

'Nothing? No, that is going too far. But perhaps not much. But you have one big financial asset. You are English. . . .'

'Is that such a help?'

'Is that a help, he asks.' He rolled his eyes. 'I can tell you right away. It is certainly *beschert* (ordained) that we met. Don't you think that the *Ribbono Shel Olam* (the Lord of the Universe) knows what he is doing? First my brother in Spain, and then me. Don't you think these things are arranged?'

'They may be.'

'They *may* be,' he mocked. 'They *are*. I can prove it. As it happens I am arranging something right now where I need an Englishman. There are other things too, but this is one to start with. I need an agent in England, or rather an English office. I want to do business there.'

'I'm not much of a businessman.'

'You would have nothing to do. Just have an office, or an address. We could export there if there was someone like you I could rely on. I have inquired. You would have to get a permit from the Board of Trade in England. Do you know anybody at the Board of Trade personally you could talk to? That is always a great help.'

I laughed: 'I daresay I could find someone,' I said. 'But what do you want to export? Oranges?'

'*Oranges*? Of course not. Oranges are for the growers, and the co-operatives. That's a different sort of business. And besides, England can get oranges from Spain, from South Africa. No, no. We must think of something personal for the people of England—something special from Palestine. And do you know what? Holy water. There are forty or fifty million Christians in

Britain. If only one per cent bought a bottle of Holy Water a year—say at Christmas-time to give as a Christmas present—that would be 50,000 bottles a year. Suppose we sold it for two shillings and sixpence a bottle. I have worked out that it would cost no more than sixpence for the bottle and transport—the water is free, from the Jordan. So we make two shillings profit a bottle, and that alone would be £5,000 profit. Not bad, eh? And suppose we only sold half that amount, that's still £2,500. Not a bad start.'

'Not bad at all,' I agreed. 'But do you think that the Christians would like to buy Holy Water from Shapiro and Company? Doesn't sound quite right somehow.'

'Shapiro and Company? Who says it will be Shapiro? I have a Christian Arab who works for me here. The English love the Arabs. We'll have his picture on each bottle, with a nice big cross.'

'Still seems a little thin for an export business,' I said. 'You need something to go with it, don't you?'

'Ahah! And you say you are not a businessman! You put your finger on it right away. Certainly we need something else, and I have that too. You know about the Dead Sea water, all the hundreds of chemicals in it. I have the figures. Ordinary seawater has four or five per cent salt, and the Dead Sea water has twenty-five per cent solids in it—nitrates, sulphur, bitumen, every kind of chemical.'

'But there are already big chemical factories there, aren't there?'

'Of course there are. I'm not in that kind of business. But I have an idea. For schoolboys. You have studied chemistry at school. They give you powders to analyse for a test. It is prepared in the school laboratory. It is a bore. But suppose a schoolboy could be given for a birthday present—or a Christmas present—a large bottle of Dead Sea water to analyse at home. He gets a nice bottle, with a map of Palestine on it, and there's a sealed envelope telling him all the chemicals he should be able to detect, and the quantities. I sell it by itself, or with a home chemical set. But think of the difference. A *"Home* Chemical Set", or a *"Dead Sea* Chemical Set". Can you see what an idea it is?'

I looked at him with some admiration. 'It's absolutely wonderful,' I said. 'But would you be allowed to fill your bottles?'

He moved his head slowly from side to side in a deprecating way. 'How much would we need? They would never miss it. Of course we have to do it quietly. No need to draw attention. As a matter of fact I have a cousin who has a small bathing place and café on the shore. It could be done. And wouldn't it be very good Zionist publicity?'

I had to laugh again at his enthusiasm. 'I'm not sure about Zionist publicity, but I love the idea of a Dead Sea Chemical Set. All the same, I'm sorry, Yitzchak, I'm the wrong man. I haven't really come here for business.'

'All right,' he said engagingly. 'You need time to think about it. I have something else that goes with it. Very good for you. But that can wait. But tell me. What kind of book are you writing? I suppose it's about the new Jewish Homeland, to sell to Zionists. Why shouldn't that make you a little money?'

'Oh, it's not that kind of a book at all, I'm afraid.'

'Then why have you come here to write?'

His interest was impossible to resist. 'I'm writing about the origin of the Midrash, and its relation to the early synagogues here in Palestine,' I said. 'At least I'd *like* to make it as broad as that if I can find some useful material. What I'd like to find is some old manuscripts, some inscription, something from that period that would throw light on the subject. But I haven't the faintest idea how to start looking. Of course I've been talking in a general way to the people at the University. . . .'

He was listening with mounting excitement. 'But this is fantastic!' he said. 'Quite fantastic. Why didn't you tell me you were a scholar? You said you were a writer. I thought a journalist. Listen. Only last week when I was down at the Dead Sea my cousin Hermann told me he'd heard a rumour from some Bedouins down there that they had some very old parchments for sale—old writing that they'd found in a cave. But who can believe an Arab? Maybe it's something they manufacture—for tourists. But if you *understand* these things. . . .'

'I'm no expert,' I said, 'but I know something about old

JERUSALEM

scripts.' I felt my own excitement growing. 'Do you think that we could ask your cousin. . . ?'

Shapiro suddenly got cautious. 'It's no good to rush. We must think. There are two possibilities.' He fell into a Talmudic sing-song. 'If they are real old manuscripts—really valuable—we don't want any excitement. That Hermann is not too easy at times. We have to consider. And if they're false, what's the hurry?'

I had to laugh. I could see that he might have some other see-saw argument in his mind. If they are genuine, why let this Englishman into things? Or was I being unfair? I thought I would tease him.

'Perhaps I could ask someone at the University,' I said. 'Some expert . . .'

He rose to the bait with a swift protest. 'No, no. Not yet. I will inquire quietly from Hermann. These Bedouin. They are here one day and gone for months. We will see. If we need an expert, I know an old rabbi here I could ask. . . .'

Ah well, I thought. Shapiro's Holy Water. We rose to go and he held out his hand. 'So we are partners,' he said warmly. 'For this I must thank Yossilë. You will think about the agency in England?'

'I'll think about it. But somehow it doesn't seem quite right for me. But for the flat I must really thank you. It's wonderful.'

His round cheeks glowed with appreciation. '*Hakol b'seder*: everything O.K. You will see. Now I have some business to do. Immigration. Trouble. Nothing but trouble. I have to go to Haifa. But if you need anything, let me know. And you must come to my house anyway. You must meet my wife. I will be in touch with you when I get back.'

* * *

I looked in at the hotel for the post. The card had arrived for the High Commissioner's reception, and there was a letter also from a settlement in northern Galilee—Kfar Haran. I knew who this letter was from and opened it quickly. It was rather as if in the first week or so in Jerusalem I had been sitting quietly at the table while the cards were being dealt, and now I was picking them up rapidly to see my hand.

I read the letter, and putting it, with the card, into my pocket, set out for the bus to go up to the University. It was a short letter, from Malcah. I had written to her to say that I was in Jerusalem, and this was her reply, inviting me to come and see her and her family and the settlement they lived in. No talk of Crusaders' Castles or funny hats for the spring: just a blunt unaffected note saying how pleased she was that I had come at last to see *Haaretz* (the Land). She would like to show me everything. She wondered if I had changed. 'So much else has changed in England. . . .'

It was now ten years since I had met her in Florence. She had never understood then, coming from Poland, how a Jewish boy, with a background apparently similar to her own, could be travelling on holiday as the protégé of his Christian headmaster —and with Sedgewick a clergyman, too—a *priest*. For me it had been equally amazing that a young girl, who might have been my sister or my cousin, could be caught up in such a web of intrigue, travelling to Palestine on a false passport and sharing the immigration visa it contained with a strange man as his supposed wife. It was sad that the closeness we had shared in Florence—that brief encounter—had almost evaporated over the years. Was it the way she always wrote about the British? I agreed with all her criticisms of British policy in Palestine, but I suppose I resented the harshness with which she wrote—her unwillingness to allow that the British had any problem—or any virtue—at all. She had sent me a snapshot after her first child had been born and I had seen what the hard life of the settlement had made of her—rough, solid, unattractive. Years of silence had passed since then: it was time I saw her again. Perhaps some of my own nightmares would blow away in the realism that I had seen in the background of the snapshot—the small ugly buildings, the rocky soil, the watchtower with its constant guard. . . .

As I walked through the hot street thinking how to arrange

the journey, some of my personal mix-up seemed to float away. Perhaps it was the idea of going north to Galilee that brought back, as always, the excitement of going north as a schoolboy from the flat softness of my school in the south to our home in Prescott. Would the air be crisp and heartening? Was there always some magic in the north, some hard courage that sprang out of the mountains, breeding a race of men—like the Scots—who had a passion to believe as well as to fight? It was easy enough to credit this if one thought back to the history of Galilee—'Galilee of the Gentiles'—wild men who clung to their ancient paganism against the cult of Judaea, but having once accepted the new beliefs filled them with the same pagan force—zealots like John of Gishchalav who led the fight against the Romans—men with a sense of mystery who wanted to believe in a Messiah. . . .

I could find it all, no doubt, in George Adam Smith, but as I walked I thought suddenly instead of a verse in the Bible, where Jacob, on his deathbed, is giving each of his twelve sons an oracular blessing. It was the blessing of the son who would live in the north that came into my head: *Naphtali is a hind let loose*. . . . I began to chant the blessings to myself—Naphtali, Joseph, Benjamin—as I had chanted them so often in the weekly reading in synagogue:

Naphtali is a hind let loose, he giveth goodly words. Joseph is a fruitful bough—a fruitful bough by a well, whose branches run over the wall. . . .

Oh, that flowering branch! I could feel it everywhere around me—the orange blossom, the bougainvillaea. . . . *Benjamin shall ravin as a wolf.* . . . I walked along singing, looking at everyone in the street as if they were old friends.

The sunshine seemed to fill me. So much lay ahead. It was Wednesday, with the High Commissioner's party on Thursday. I would go up to Kfar Haran as soon as I could after it. Perhaps I could get Dov to drive me there in his Buick. I would see Malcah and her world with fresh eyes.

It was good to be out in the street, jostling with the cheerful crowd, fighting one's way into the bus, ready for the rough bumpy ride to Mount Scopus, sweeping past the old bearded Jews of Mea Shearim and the Nashashibi houses which followed, up and up to the magic view from the mountain. There was so much waiting to be discovered—including, of course, Yael.

★ ★ ★

I would have enjoyed the party anyhow. I was in the mood to let things come to me; and how could one resist the fun of that kind of evening—the British abroad at their most bizarre—the uniforms, the flunkeys, the Bokhara wall-hangings, the royal portraits, the babel of tongues, the marvellous mix-up of people —bald high-domed Jews, plump Dominican priests, fiery-eyed Arabs with pencil-thin moustaches, flat-chested Englishwomen in black chiffon, Oriental wives in long coloured robes—the unseen ever-present Raj, the miracle of our being there, high-up above the Temple, the richness of roots, the clash of wills. . . .

But it wasn't this at all, once I had seen Yael: or rather it was all this transformed by the strangest feeling—a peculiar surge of happiness inside me. The whole party seemed to glow—to smile—with her radiance. I wandered round, glass in hand, exchanging greetings with people I knew from the University, being introduced, being buttonholed; but always out of the corner of my eye I was trying to see where she was, to get back to where I could look at her again from across the room and let her beauty run slowly through me.

Briscombe had been waiting at the door to help with the introductions to the High Commissioner. He was tall, with a lock of fair hair falling over one eye—gawky and friendly. It was he, taking me round, who had introduced me briefly to a Mr and Mrs Sirov, the man looking about fifty, grey-haired and gentle, his wife much younger, dark and passionate, with a faint remote smile in her eyes. When we left them and moved on he had made the expected remark: 'Isn't she terrific?' 'Yes,' I had agreed slowly, 'terrific'; but we had been whisked on, and soon after he had left me for other guests. I had stood for a while where he left me, in a dream.

JERUSALEM

He had come back briefly at one point to introduce a lean handsome Englishman whom I would have expected to be a Colonel—he had the regulation clipped look, with a well-brushed head of steel-grey hair; but he turned out to be a high official of the Police—Inspector Hardcastle. To my surprise it was apparently the Inspector who had sought the introduction, but I soon understood why.

'Briscombe tells me we were at the same College,' he said breezily, giving me a clean firm handshake. 'Somewhat after my time, I expect.'

Heather again. She certainly had told her cousin 'all about me', even to the detail of my College. Trust an English civil servant to be thorough. I exchanged a few college pleasantries with the Inspector, but was not too much at ease. He was one of those Englishmen who seem quite cold at the centre. Clear, rather small grey eyes look at you with a slightly ruthless detachment. Sentiment seems out. But perhaps one has it wrong. This one was friendly enough, firmly and very sensibly resisting Briscombe's efforts to get him into the drama group.

'I don't know why people are being so difficult,' Briscombe was saying. 'It's going to be terrific. We're doing *The Importance of Being Earnest*,' he said to me. 'But I want to produce it in quite an unusual way. Don't you think Hardcastle would make an excellent Algie?'

'Couldn't get to rehearsals, old boy,' Hardcastle said comfortably. 'Just a little too busy at night.' Was there after all a twinkle in those eyes?

Briscombe turned back to me. 'But *you're* not busy,' he said. 'I'm sure you'd enjoy it.'

'How are you producing it?' I asked, as Hardcastle drifted off.

Briscombe was all too ready to explain. 'I'd like to produce it as a pantomime,' he said. 'It's no good treating it for the dialogue: they wouldn't understand. But panto is our great invention, and this would lend itself to it perfectly. Can't you see it? Lady Bracknell played by a man, and the two girls played by young boys—one Arab and one Jewish. Bound to make them laugh. In any case, it's very hard to get hold of Arab women, and everything here has to be one of each, with some English mixed in, like the Legislative Council. Perhaps it's better not to have Hardcastle as Algie,' he said reflectively. 'Better to aim at an Arab for John and a Jew for Algie. After all, they end up in the play as brothers. Don't you think it will be fun?'

I looked at him with some wonder. 'Fun?'

An idea suddenly struck him. 'I wonder how you'd be as Miss Prism,' he began.

'Not Miss Prism,' I said firmly.

'Well, how about the Rev. Chasuble?'

'I will come and see the play,' I said. 'I will buy tickets. I will sell programmes at the door in the cause of Arab-Jewish amity. But Chasuble? No.'

He shook his head sadly and moved off. There were other guests to take care of. Happy to be let off I looked round for the Sirovs, and felt a sudden emptiness to see that they were no longer there. It was absurd. I had a sense almost of panic to think they might have left. I wandered into another room and drew a deep breath of relief to see them again.

A young attaché came up and began to talk. With enormous casualness I asked him, nodding slightly towards them, if I had their names right. I found myself trembling as he began to talk of them. 'Yes, Sirov,' he said. 'Alexander Sirov. He's a famous plant geneticist—a Russian. Wonderful man. They say he's done marvels on orange-growing.'

'And Mrs Sirov?'

'Hard to say, isn't it? She could be Egyptian, couldn't she? Not European, anyhow. Marvellous-looking woman, isn't she?'

Yes, I thought. She could be Egyptian—ancient Egyptian. Standing quietly by her husband, she was as remote and mysterious as Nefertite. Her strong black hair gave her head the look of that ancient princess, setting off a high wide brow and enormous brown eyes. Every feature of her face was shaped and cut with sculptured strength and delicacy—the high cheekbones, the straight nose, the slightly parted graceful lips. Her dark olive skin glowed with a hidden fire, and the same power seemed to flow from her in the way she stood—not slender but round and rooted in the earth, like a Maillol.

There had been a group of people with them, but now they were alone, and I caught Sirov's eye on me. I went over and was greeted by him with that wonderful natural courtesy which is for a certain kind of Russian Jew the supreme mark of their caste.

'I was hoping to see more of you,' he said. 'I have such pleasant memories of Oxford. I was there soon after the war. It is changed now, they say. They make motor-cars. But I hope nothing has really changed. Reassure me.'

'The centre hasn't changed,' I said. 'It's like the Old City.'

He smiled. 'But without a Wailing Wall, eh?' He turned to his wife. 'It's so very beautiful, Yael,' he said. 'I must take you there one day.'

Standing so close to her had the strangest effect on me. My knees felt weak. I had no idea at all if I showed it.

'Are you lecturing at the University here?' she asked. She had a low, rather vibrant voice, with something like a French accent.

I laughed. 'Oh dear no. I'm nothing like good enough for that. I'm listening to lectures, and writing a bit.'

I told them about my flat and where it was, and they both laughed. 'Why, you're our neighbour,' Sirov said. 'We live only two streets away. We have an Arab house too, of course. They are really wonderful, are they not? Bernstein has the right idea. He builds ultra-modern houses for other people and lives in an Arab house himself. Very sensible man.'

Now that we were talking I could see the softness in her eyes. 'We are going away on Sunday for a couple of days,' she said, 'but will you come and see us next Thursday, a week from tonight? We are having some people in to supper, at seven.'

She told me the address. We talked for a few minutes more and they left. I could have taken a lift back with them, as my neighbours, but Briscombe had offered to drive me home and I was somehow glad of the break. I went to get myself a strong whisky and ask myself what it all meant. Not that I could put it to myself in words. It was more like taking my temperature. Perhaps

I *had* a temperature. I felt myself burning, as if the glow in her body had filled me.

* * *

It was good to wake up the next morning and feel for a moment that I had had a strange compelling dream. Now that I was waking up, I was alone and myself, and the world was real again. Still only half awake I started some coffee and threw open the shutter a little to let the sun stream in where it wouldn't dazzle me. Staggering with the coffee across the cool marble floor towards the table, I sat down thankfully, but there to confound me were the scrawled drafts and the final short clearly-written version of the poem that had forced itself out of me when I got home. I picked it up wonderingly. I had never written a poem in my life to anybody. Was it really about her? It seemed to be more about the beauty of nature, with something in it about a bough by a well; and as I read it I could feel the image grow in me again of a woman who drew her life and strength out of the earth, like a tree.

Like a tree! *Asherah, Astarte*—like all those sacred groves that the Jews in the Bible are commanded to cut down ruthlessly if they want God to love them. *For I am a jealous God,* he kept saying. Why was he so jealous, so quick to anger—like my father, whose dignified bearded face grew black with anger if he found that I had been playing in the park when I should have been doing my Hebrew lessons. *For ye shall destroy their altars and break their images and cut down their groves . . . and ye shall burn their groves with fire and hew down the graven images of their gods.* Week after week, year after year, the iniquity of it all had been drummed into me—the 'high places' and the groves, and all the pleasures and picnics of that carefree world outside the Jewish schoolroom. *The sin of Judah is written with a pen of iron,* Jeremiah had said, *and with the point of a diamond. It is graven upon the table of their heart.* And what did this heart-searing sin amount to? Why, the most charming of thoughts: *That their children remember their altars and their groves by the green trees upon the high*

JERUSALEM

hills. My God! Surely even Jeremiah, when he said words like this, had been moved by something other than anger. *The green trees upon the high hills*—there's love and happiness in it. I liked it anyhow, and I saw now what I had meant in the poem I had written for Yael.

I heard a car drive up. There was a knock at the door and there was Dov, burly, swarthy, and radiating goodwill. I had asked Shapiro before he left if Dov might be free to do a journey to Galilee some day soon, and he had come to tell me that he had just arranged to drive an American couple—tourists—on the usual run, Tiberias, the Valley of Jezreel, Safed. Did I want to come? They were leaving on Sunday.

I accepted willingly and asked him in for a cup of coffee. My conversational Hebrew still creaked a little, and though his English was not bad—good enough for a tourist guide—we found it easier to talk in German. I told him that I wanted to stay for a day or so at Kfar Haran, and he readily worked out a plan by which I could be left there one morning and picked up on the return journey the following afternoon. I should be back in Jerusalem by Thursday afternoon, as I wanted to be.

As we drank our coffee, I asked him what he had done in Roumania before coming to Palestine. He had worked in a vineyard, he said. His family had lived in the village close to these vineyards for several generations. It was a lovely village on the slopes of the Carpathians—and as he talked he grew lyrical for its remembered beauty. I was to find this often in Palestine—the nostalgic memories of the immigrants for an idealized youth —Europe without the pogroms. 'But here,' I asked him, 'you prefer not to work on the land?'

He grinned rather endearingly. 'It's better money,' he said, 'and I like meeting people. Besides I do a lot of work for Shapiro —many different things.' It sounded as though it were better not to ask what.

After he had gone I started getting out my papers, wondering if I could start organizing a routine for working in the flat. But alone, my thoughts went back immediately to Yael. Briscombe had told me something more about them as he drove me home.

Sirov, apart from being a famed geneticist, with valuable experimental orchards which had made him rich, was also an important political figure. He had taken a strong position on the need for the Jews to work in harmony—indeed in unity—with the Arabs. For this he was naturally hated by the zealots among both Jews and Arabs. Even the Government, approving his views in theory, found him an uncomfortable person to work with, and difficult to give support to. The Government had to work through community leaders. They could hardly work through a man—or a group—who wanted to break down community barriers. 'It's funny,' Briscombe had said. 'You'd think it suited us. We're supposed to like compromise. But it doesn't. We like him personally. He's a marvellous man, don't you think? But we don't know what to do with him.'

And his wife? Was she active in the same group? No, he said. She didn't play any part in politics. But she must do something, I insisted. I could hardly imagine her just as a housewife. Briscombe had given me a look. Obviously everybody wanted to know what lay behind that mysterious mask. He had been told that she was a sculptress, he said. They were a wonderful couple. Yes, I could see that.

I might have asked him if he knew where she came from, but this was something that lay, as it were, privately between me and her as Jews. The French accent could mean anything in the Middle East, except probably a French origin. That dark brooding beauty was timeless and placeless—Egypt, Spain, Turkey—she could have come from any of these places, or all at once.

With paper before me and pen in hand I tried to turn my thoughts to the Midrash, but it was easier to start again on a poem. There was something about her, apart from her beauty, that I wanted to get down. Was it the Earth Goddess in her that made one tremble, or was I already thinking of her as the Yael of the Book of Judges, driven by more than gentleness? Even at that moment I knew that beauty of that kind cannot exist casually in a woman: it must in some sense be all-consuming. And yet the tenderness in her eyes. . . . There was a light knock at the door, and as if by some miracle of my will, she stood there, smiling.

'I thought I must welcome you as our neighbour,' she said lightly, coming in and drawing off her gloves. 'Do you need any help? Have you got a girl to come and clean for you?'

I felt as if some great weight had lifted from me. I knew now that we would be friends. Instead of the drive and the fever, there was a great happy calm inside me. I had no need to say anything. She had understood and accepted me.

She was looking round in an amused way at the pile of books and papers. 'You have made yourself at home very quickly,' she said. 'It's very nice here, isn't it?'

The poem that I had written was still lying on the table. I offered it to her and she took it over to the window to sit down and read it. I lit a cigarette as I saw her look through it once quickly, and then read it over again more carefully. 'What difficult handwriting you have,' she said smilingly. 'I like the poem. It's really the first Psalm, isn't it?' She murmured the words of the Psalm softly in Hebrew. '*Like a tree planted on the river bank, which yields its fruit in season and whose leaves never fade.*' She looked up. 'Can I keep it?'

'It was for you.'

'Yes, I know.' She put it in her bag. 'I will read it again later. I don't understand English too well, you know.' She smiled. 'I mean the exact weight of words in a poem.'

We talked for a minute or two and she began to put her gloves on, ready to go. I noticed, as I had the night before, the great care with which she dressed, especially the strong solid colours she wore—a light loose coat of some fine dark purple wool, a small yellow hat that lit up her black hair and big brown eyes. 'I am going in to my studio,' she said. 'I thought I'd walk as it's such a glorious day. Are you free to come?'

As we set out she said, as if reading my thought: 'I'm not very suitably dressed for walking. But I have a lunch at the King David. I'll just look in at the studio to see what I did yesterday. One can never tell till the next day.'

It was odd the way she walked, with a kind of springy vitality, almost as if she were a soldier. Perhaps it was just the energy in her, but it seemed almost as if she were in training. She talked easily about houses we passed and people whom they brought to mind. She asked about my work and background; and when in turn I asked how long she had lived in Jerusalem, she told me about her family.

'We are Sephardim, of course,' she said. 'We have lived in these countries—Egypt, Salonika, Syria, and here in Palestine since we left Spain in the twelfth century. Of course there's one thing you might not guess.' She turned her head to smile at me. 'For a long time we had a kind of British nationality. Ironic, isn't it? We got protection from the British Consulate in the middle of the last century when they had a policy of helping Jews who were in trouble, mostly Russian Jews but others too. Of course it was just a way of showing that the British were masters everywhere they wanted to be. Still, it was good in its way. It helped us for a time. There had been a big law case. The head of our family—it must have been my great-grandfather—was killed by some Arabs near Tiberias over a property dispute. We needed help. The British Consul gave it.'

'How long did you stay British?'

'Oh, quite a long time. If one got a piece of paper, one clung to it. I think my father was still British. Anyhow, he repaid the debt.' She was silent for a moment, and I waited.

'He worked for the British at the beginning of the war,' she said finally. 'Secretly. The Turks caught him in 1915 and threw him into prison, in Acre. He was tortured, and was a broken man when he came out. He died soon after. My mother and all the children had moved to Beirut in the meantime to be near her family. They had French nationality, so we became French.'

'And now?'

'Oh now,' she said with a trace of mockery, 'now everything is solved. I am Ivrith—Hebrew. And the British are our masters again. Ah well, this is history, I suppose.'

'You don't really like us, do you?'

She burst into a delighted laugh. 'I like *you*,' she said. 'I even like some English *non*-Jews. Am I supposed to like everybody? Do *you* like everybody?'

I had to laugh with her. 'I like all Sephardim,' I said happily. 'Especially the Yemenites, I think.' We were passing a couple in the street, with their long robes and little black hats setting off their curly-bearded faces. 'Everything seems so pale in England when I look at this.'

We were approaching a rather squalid area close to the Old City. As always it was the Arabs one was aware of—their hoarse argument, the dirt, the smell, the noise of hammers, the calls and blows to camels and donkeys. 'I even like this,' I said.

'Yes, you like it—all Englishmen do. Look at it.' She waved her arm. 'It's like a chain around us. Sometimes I hate it—hate it. But the British want it all to stay, don't they? So picturesque, isn't it?'

'But isn't this the world you're used to?'

We had reached a building which had a small picture-framing shop in front, with a door hidden at the side, opening into a dark hall with stairs. There were some rooms on a landing and then, after some more stairs, a door which opened quite unexpectedly into a large dazzlingly white studio—a huge low divan at one end, a profusion of rugs, some old lamps, lumps of stone and clay, and a number of pieces of sculpture. 'This is the world I am used to,' she said, throwing her hat and coat on to the divan and walking over to a stand where some large object was covered with a cloth. She lifted the cloth and looked at her work for a few minutes silently. I heard her mutter: 'Oh God.' Then, putting the cloth back, she turned to me, smiling. 'Well, it was a good walk. Shall I make you some coffee—real coffee—Turkish coffee?'

I had been looking at the work around me—some strongly carved heads in stone and some clay busts, including one of her husband—a good likeness, but dead. There was more life in some animal heads she had carved in a less realistic way, but all the work seemed to me derived and secondary, as if it were an expression of some other energy that burned in her.

'You don't like my work, do you?' she said, laughing at my

confusion. 'I have a secret to tell you. I don't like it either. I know the difference, you see. But I *can* make good coffee.'

It was fun that she could be so straight. Obviously the sight of her work under the cloth had made her dissatisfied, but she was not heavy about it. There was a kind of mischievousness in her eyes, very different from the momentary sadness earlier when she had talked of her father, and from her remoteness of the night before. I said:

'Something has made you very gay this morning, hasn't it? I'm quite sure you're not always like this. What is it?'

'It's you, I think,' she said laughing. 'I'm glad you're here. You're such a comfortable person to know. But *you're* not always like this either, are you?'

I had to smile wryly. 'No, I don't think I am.'

'Good. I'm glad you're human, like the rest of us.' She was bending over the coffee, but now she turned and looked at me. 'You *are* human,' she said gently.

I stood there in silence, and she walked over to me and took my hand. Then very slowly—almost deliberately—she raised her head and kissed me softly on the lips. It was neither casual nor voracious. Her lips simply lay on mine in utter sweetness.

But she was not smiling when she stood back after a minute, and I held her hands. Looking closely into her eyes, I saw what I had not seen before—the beginning, the faint trace of something driven, almost haggard. And yet there was such softness in her mouth, a sweetness that seemed to melt into me.

I was trembling and found myself murmuring the first thing that came into my head, without any thought at what it implied. 'You're like Samson's riddle to the Philistines,' I said. 'Out of the strong came forth sweetness.'

'Yes, I'm a riddle. What was the answer? I've forgotten it.'

But I had just remembered the answer and wished I had been silent. 'Oh, it's nothing,' I said. 'It just came into my head.'

'Ah, if it was unconscious you really must tell me. Didn't Delilah worm the answer out of Samson?' She was holding my hands at full length and laughing at me. 'I feel like Delilah.'

JERUSALEM

'It was something he saw on the road to Gath,' I said reluctantly. 'A dead lion with a swarm of bees in the carcass.'

'Ah yes, a dead lion.' She drew a deep sigh and was silent. But then the smile came back into her eyes. 'You poor dear,' she said affectionately. 'You really must stop reading the Bible.' She gave me a gentle kiss on the cheek and went across to pick up the coffee, now ready. We sipped it slowly, saying nothing, and then, as if taking a decision, she put on a long overall ready to do some work. As I rose to go she stood beside me for a minute and touched my face gently with her fingers. 'You're so wonderfully innocent,' she said.

'*Innocent!*'

'Oh yes, innocent, innocent. Don't change.'

As I opened the door to go, I turned for a last look at her. She had already started taking the cloth off the work on the stand. She looked up with great tenderness.

★ ★ ★

All I care to remember of the American couple is the way they forced Dov and me into the friendship and understanding of conspirators. There was nothing wrong with them. Their excitement at what they saw, old and new, was completely justified and predictable. But after the first day Dov and I, without exchanging a word on the subject, knew what we knew about each other's thoughts.

As a guide Dov had the history of the places and monuments we saw very pat, and in workmanlike English. I never added any information from my own studies, but he knew what it all meant to me. And we talked to each other in a kind of shorthand, without barriers.

'How will it all end?' I said to him one night as we sat alone, drinking coffee, on the tiny terrace of the new hotel on the top of the mountain above Safed. We had been talking about the political situation.

'Some bloody fight,' he said morosely. 'It will start in Europe and spread here. All we can do is to get ready.'

'You don't think the British can keep the peace?'

He laughed. 'The British seem to me like the Hapsburgs in 1914. They can't see what's happening to their Empire. They think that God ordained it so it must last for ever. Even British Jews are infected. Take yourself. What will you get out of coming here? Some memory of *Cheder* (Hebrew school)—some material for your studies—and then you'll go back to being an Englishman.'

'I wonder. Strange things happen to one here.' I stood up and walked to the edge of the balcony with its distant view over Samaria towards the mountains of Judaea. Behind the song of the crickets, there was a faint breeze rustling the trees of the wooded slope below us. The air was very fresh and perfumed, and the sky was light with its thick cluster of stars. The unutterable beauty simply forced the thought of Yael into my mind. I was due at Kfar Haran the next morning, but all that I was seeing and hoped to see kept fading at a moment like this against the longing to be back in Jerusalem.

And so it was even when I saw Malcah and the vigorous, fearless world that she and her family were building. If I were writing of Malcah now there would be so much more to say. One had to see a settlement and stay there, to know what the Yishuv meant. As we examined the herd of cows, the fields of wheat and barley, the crude dining-hall with its rows of wooden tables, and the small hut that she and her husband had as their own, I felt moved, as anybody would, at the honesty and courage of it all. It was uncomplicated and inspiring. It was easy to understand that they would die—as indeed Malcah did—to defend what they had built and won out of rock and desert. I was deeply moved and yet, in a most painful way, a stranger.

The true marvel was the children, but there was a good moment too when Malcah took me across a couple of fields to show me the special treasure of the settlement—a tiny relic of an old synagogue, going back to the third century A.D. which they had uncovered when ploughing up the land and which they continued to work at, with a holy zeal, in all their spare time. All that they had found was a few square feet of a mosaic pavement decorated with the usual Galilee design of birds and fishes. Everything else, it seemed, had crumbled and blown away. But it was enough to know that something in the soil itself linked them with their ancestors.

I remembered how Malcah and I had walked around Florence together and how she had looked with tears at the rich European beauty that she loved so much and was exchanging for rock and sand. But she had found something here more precious to her than all that I clung to.

I talked about this to Dov as we drove back on Thursday morning towards Jerusalem. I told him also how I had hoped at the beginning to find something myself that could bring my dusty studies to life, and how Shapiro had hinted that he could help.

Dov's swarthy face, his heavy-lidded eyes concentrating on the winding road ahead, broke into a grin. 'That Shapiro,' he said. 'You only have to mention something you want and he'll get it for you—especially for money.'

'He said his cousin Hermann had heard rumours of things discovered in caves near the Dead Sea.'

'Maybe he has, maybe he hasn't. But if you've started Shapiro on the track you'll get your manuscript. Perhaps it won't actually date back to the rabbinic times—maybe it will be a good fifty years old—but it will be something nice to take back to England.'

'He wants me to go into business with him,' I said. 'Do you think we would get on?'

'Listen,' he said. 'I love Yitzchak; but for you to go into business with him, that is another matter. The kind of business we do isn't always—what shall I say?—easy for an Englishman. It all depends on the country you live in. There's an atmosphere about it. You do things in one country you just wouldn't do in another.'

I made no comment and he drove on, with the stony hills winding and unwinding under the bright blue sky. 'What's legal?' he said after a while. 'What's illegal? I will tell you what we do. Sometimes we get things from Syria, or take things into Syria or Egypt without informing everybody. All right. It's against the law. But the whole law here is illegal. Palestine was promised to the Jews as a National Home. It's in the Balfour Declaration. Well, is it a National Home, or is it just a British colony? You tell *me*.'

He was not angry, just ruminating on life. It was as if the desire he felt to explain things to me had stimulated him to express things he usually took for granted. He would be silent for a while, or turn to point out to the Americans sitting quietly behind something that we were passing near the road, and then he would turn back to me in quiet German.

'Don't get the wrong idea,' he said. 'The law is the law, and most people here have no reason to go against it. As a matter of fact the Jews love the law—well, *you* should know that. Isn't the Talmud all about the law? I've never studied it but that's what I've always been told. And another thing. The Jews like the way the British have set up a legal system here. It's very good—very fair. And the Arabs like it too. You know how Jewish lawyers always act for Arabs in law cases. In the courts everything seems good. The law is above ordinary quarrels. That's good. All the same, one can't always put it above life itself.'

'I think it says that in the Talmud, doesn't it?' he asked. 'Take the law of Shabbat. Mustn't do this, mustn't do that. But to save life you can do anything. Well, we feel that way too. Take immigration. There's a quota of less than a thousand for this year. Just think of that, and then think of Germany, not to mention Poland or Roumania. If we can save any extra Jews from Germany and bring them in, it has to be done illegally. Do you think any Jew would feel guilty at that? Well, perhaps only an English Jew would.'

'Poor old English,' I said. 'We get it from all sides.'

'Well, you deserve it,' he said comfortably. 'The fact is, you haven't had to face the problem. Just as well for you. I know how you'd react if you had to consider helping an illegal immigrant.'

'So that's part of Shapiro's business,' I said. 'Gun-running too, I wouldn't doubt.'

'Well, it's a nice powerful car,' he said, patting the wheel affectionately. 'I will say one thing for the Americans . . .' he lowered his voice when he mentioned the word, '. . . they do know how to make cars. Yes, we've done quite a bit in our time. And I hope we'll do more.'

'The mystery to me is how Shapiro can keep all these different things going at once,' I said. 'I can only do one thing at a time, but he seems like a conjurer, keeping so many balls in the air.'

Dov laughed. 'You don't even begin to know how many things he does. And not even the kind of man he really is,' he added. He was silent for a while, as if debating whether to tell me something. 'I laugh at him,' he went on, 'but of course I wouldn't work with him if I didn't respect him. Take money, for example—the way he earns his money. There's profit in what we do. There has to be. So he does it all for money, eh?'

'There's something else, you mean.'

'Yes, there's something else. I want to tell you, though I don't want him to know I told you. He puts on this act of always looking for ways of making money, and it's quite true. He likes money. He enjoys making it. But what does he do with it? He gives most of it away—he and his wife—to support a home for orphan refugee girls that they run in Haifa. There's a reason for that too. His own sister.'

It was almost unnecessary to say another word. The details of how it had happened didn't matter. But Dov filled in a little as we drove along. It was an anachronism, really. Later it would have been formalized in a concentration camp story. But with Shapiro it had been premature—unnecessary—even unusual. His sister had been attacked and raped by some young Nazi hooligans. Soon after—perhaps without any direct connection— she had died, at eighteen. This was how Shapiro and his wife kept her memory. With no children of their own, they had already brought ten young girls in, by any illegal method possible, and kept them for an interim stage in a private house in Haifa run by a woman friend. There were always three or four girls there at a time settling down and learning a little Hebrew, after which they were passed discreetly into Kibbutzim. It was all arranged and paid for by Shapiro—just one of his little businesses which, like all the others, he preferred to keep to himself.

Somehow it brought a picture to my mind of Malcah in Florence as a young girl and Malcah now, rough and solid, but very tender towards her children and the little mosaic of their third-century synagogue. She had shown me some old coins they had found too—battered, irregularly shaped little coins of Bar Cochba's time, with a crude *Menorah* on one side and some scratchy Hebrew letters on the obverse. I would have liked to have had one to carry with me—a *pruta*, no doubt—a farthing. It was a word which was just as sweet and affectionate in Hebrew as in English.

* * *

The first person I saw at the Sirov party was Inspector Hardcastle, lean and sardonic as ever, and wearing our old College tie. 'Have to cling to tradition here,' he said apologetically. 'I never owned one at Oxford, but it seems right, somehow, to wear one abroad. Showing the flag.'

His tone was faintly puzzling. It was hard to imagine anyone who needed an external symbol less than he did to show that he was an Englishman. Perhaps it was aimed somehow at me. Was I letting the side down? But he didn't linger on it.

'Has Briscombe lined you up for the play?' he asked cheerfully. 'I imagine he wants you for the Rev. Chasuble.'

'That's a very kind guess,' I said, 'but the position is much worse. He really wants me for Miss Prism.'

Hardcastle's eyebrows rose slightly, and at that moment Yael came up to greet us. She was very different in her own home from the remote mysterious woman who had stood by her husband's side at Government House. Here, there was an active warmth and tenderness in her eyes for everybody. It was Hardcastle this time whose laconic manner seemed remote. As for me, my heart turned over merely to be near her.

Her husband came up. It was he, it seemed, who had invited Hardcastle, having run into him during the week at Givath

Moed, near Tel Aviv, where he maintained one of his main experimental stations. They began to talk of something he had shown Hardcastle there, and confirmed an arrangement to meet at another of the stations just north of Haifa during the following week. It became clear as they talked that Hardcastle, who had grown up on a farm, knew a lot about the subject. The conversation became technical, and Yael took me off to introduce me to the other guests.

The house itself was quite like the one I was living in, but very much larger, and furnished with rich half-Oriental elegance. The guests were highly assorted—a professor (whom I knew) from the University, a couple of Arabs and their wives, an American scientist, a woman journalist from France, two Jewish residents from Jerusalem, also with wives, and a woman painter who had recently immigrated from Germany and settled to work at Sfath (Safed). She was having a show in Jerusalem in a few weeks' time, and had come in to make the arrangements. Apart from practical things of this kind she had, it seemed, very little use for Jerusalem.

'It's all so artificial here,' she told me, in a heavy German accent. 'Politics and business and social engagements. All these new blocks of flats with modern conveniences—motor-cars and bridge parties. The whole flavour of the city is being ruined. Almost as bad as Tel Aviv. But up in Sfath, it could be the Middle Ages—like Rothenburg.'

'Why not go back and live in Rothenburg?' said one of the Jewish men standing by.

'That's not the point,' she retorted sharply. 'Sfath is Jewish—intensely Jewish, much more Jewish in its way than Jerusalem. It's uncorrupted—abstracted—all the old rabbis and their cabbalistic beliefs. . . .'

'It's all right for the rabbis,' the man said, 'but for a Jew coming to live in Palestine today, one either accepts the existence of Tel Aviv, with all its crudity, or one is out of touch with reality.'

'Tel Aviv is a miracle,' said the French journalist. 'I never saw anywhere such *joie de vivre*.'

'I'm for Haifa,' said the American scientist. 'The hill and the bay—reminds me of San Francisco. And what I like about it, to be frank, is that it's neither wholly Jewish nor wholly Arab. They seem to get on so well there. . . .'

But they seemed to get on well here too, I thought. The Arab guests, one a lawyer and the other a doctor, were talking easily, with bright smiling faces, to Sirov, the professor and two of the others. Yael went up to them and joined in the talk happily. They obviously had some subject closely in common. I wandered over and found that they were discussing ski-ing holidays in the Lebanon. The Arabs were products of the American University of Beirut, civilized and tolerant. Obviously they would never hurt a fly.

Later, as we sat in different groups after the buffet supper had been consumed, Sirov talked to me quietly but with great intensity about his political views. He had no illusions about Arab hostility. If anything he had a more desperate view than those who were for separation. His gentle courtesy was the obverse of a quiet realism and an essentially tragic view of life. One worked at one's job, knowing that the forces beneath our so-called civilized activity could overwhelm everything. For any group—or any human being—to try to force exclusive rights on anybody else was self-defeating. If there was any solution at all to the human dilemma it lay in accepting life as it was, without expecting it to conform to pre-determined rules of one's own. As he spoke, I glanced across the room at Yael, who was talking to Hardcastle. She was looking up at him, unsmiling now, as if for the moment she had left the party and was wholly absorbed in some other feeling.

* * *

But she was relaxed again when she dropped in to my flat the next morning, as I had hoped she would. Ushah, the Yemenite girl—only fifteen, I was told, but fat and luscious as a ripe peach —had just finished cleaning up. Yael looked at her approvingly as she left. 'Just perfect,' she said. 'Either some marvellous old woman to keep you in order, or a really young girl to make you feel alive.'

Her ease with me was heart-warming. In some way she seemed to count on me for a cheerful—a normal—attitude to life and yet at the same time she gave me the feeling that the normal things of life—if there were any such things—were only a foreground for her, with something unknown, and perhaps unknowable, behind. I say this now without being sure if I really felt it at the time or have only imagined it later, for at the time everything seemed so natural and assured between us. From her first moment she seemed at home in my room, and I in turn felt utterly at ease in her studio, where I met her again that afternoon, after my morning at the University. She was in her overall, working, when I arrived, and she kissed me softly when I came in. It was hardly a sister's kiss, but there was a sister's friendship in it; and when we talked it was, that day, mostly about her family and early life.

Her mother had been the dominant figure in their large family—eight children and a thousand uncles, aunts and cousins scattered through Near-Eastern lands. Mobile and uprooted as they were, it was a family nurtured in a rigid Oriental tradition of religion and ancestor-worship; and for Yael it was her mother—powerful and independent—in whom the tradition had been enshrined. Her father, busy on mysterious missions and then imprisoned in Acre for years, she had hardly known. As she told me this and saw, no doubt, a flicker of speculation in my eyes, she picked it up with a laugh. 'Of course,' she said. 'It's terribly obvious, isn't it? Alex is a father figure.' Then she sighed. 'Oh dear, if everything were as simple as that.'

We went on talking, with an ease that grew deeper as the afternoon wore on; and something in our talk, or in my looks, made her consider for a while starting a head of me. Pulling out a large sketch-book, she sat herself cross-legged on the divan, with the pad steadied with one hand at the top, and she asked me to go on talking about myself—and especially about England, in which she had a burning interest—while she did a series of quick charcoal drawings. But then she threw them away impetuously. 'I'm not really in the mood,' she said.

There was a pause: our eyes met. It was late afternoon now: something had grown in these quiet hours. I went over to the divan and put my arms around her. She was rigid and still, as if sheltering from something that frightened her. She had been close to me while we talked, but now something had come between us. She touched my face softly with her hand, and in the abstracted touch I felt how far away she had gone. Perhaps she sensed the response in me, for she turned her head, and we looked sadly at each other.

I moved away a little and took her hand. In the brimming depth of her eyes I seemed to see down into a well of feeling, deep and clouded. I had been stirred earlier, but the tenseness had left me now, and I felt only the gentlest kind of love. We were close—intolerably close perhaps in our past and in our selves. There was warmth and beauty in the air between us, but the other force in her pulled away fiercely from these quiet roots.

I thought of this later when I left her and walked for a while alone in the Old City—the shops and markets shuttered now, the daily visitors gone, and the city's own people back in possession of their courts and alleys—the priests scurrying by, the Arab women in black and dark blue robes moving gracefully through the streets with their huge earthen dishes, the wail of Hebrew prayers (for Shabbat) from the Jewish quarter, and then a clang of bells from the Church of the Holy Sepulchre. A clang of bells! I stood still for a moment, waiting for the sound of a trumpet to sign the vivid air.

★ ★ ★

Briscombe had asked me to lunch the next day at a tiny but utterly charming Armenian restaurant that he had discovered hidden away behind the Jaffa Road. By the time lunch was over we were both flown enough with wine to be able to make light of our respective troubles.

JERUSALEM

We had got off to a good start with unexpected vodka and salt-herring—un-Armenian, but effective: and then we had surrendered to an immense shashlik, flavoured, it seemed to me, with myrrh and frankincense. My own trouble—at least on the surface—was a sudden boredom with my work. It might be fun, I felt, to decipher the seal on a Hellenistic jar-handle, or a five-word inscription on one of Sukenik's ossuaries. But to go on ploughing for months through thousands of Midrashic homilies, comparing all the variants of the text and generally Buechlerizing myself beyond all recognition, seemed impossible. It was not that I was unhappy. I was restless. Briscombe had had another letter that day from Heather, obviously puzzled at my silence. She had asked if we had met, and wondered how I was getting on. The answer was simple. I was not getting on—I was idle; and as I knew very well from years (or rather centuries) of relentless indoctrination, there was nothing more disturbing and sinful than idle happiness.

But Briscombe's troubles were even more serious. He had been told that day from on high that he would have to abandon his idea of producing *The Importance of Being Earnest*, and he was still reeling from the oddity of the reason. 'Not just the Jews,' he said plaintively. 'The Arabs too. They sent in protests. They thought it was a plot by London.'

'London?'

'Oh yes: everything we do here—if I just blow my nose—is on direct orders from the Colonial Secretary. As for this play, it's just made to order once one looks at it that way. I remember joking to you about it—I mean that Worthing and Moncrieff turn out to be brothers. Well, that's what they object to. They say that as the plan for a Legislative Council is hanging fire, the Government in London tried to put on this play to ram the lesson home. In the play each man begins by trying to use the other for his own convenience. Suddenly they discover that without knowing it they are brothers, and that's why the Colonial Secretary ordered this play—just to make the Jews and the Arabs come to their senses. Oh God!' He took a good sip of his vodka and sighed heavily.

'Probably *was* the reason,' I said cheerfully. 'Damn' good analogy. I bet Ormsby-Gore wishes he'd thought of it.'

'Oh yes. And look at this.' He began to fish in his pocket. 'I brought it to show you.' He had pulled out a page from a Hebrew newspaper—a long article entitled: *The Importance of Being Honest*. 'I'm told this is what really did the trick,' he said. 'Can you make head or tail of it?'

I recognized the paper as one run by an extreme religious party, and as I began to read the article I had to smile at the familiarity of the style. 'It's pure Talmud,' I said to Briscombe. 'A really beautiful piece of argument.'

'The brother business again?'

'Yes, but much deeper. Really exposes you root and branch. Starts off by asking: why *this* play? If a play at all, why not Shakespeare?'

'Well, I suppose they have a point there.'

'But wait a minute. They say it isn't just to show the Jews and Arabs that they're brothers. It's to try and prove that the Arabs have a superior claim to Palestine.'

'Oh God! This is too much. How on earth . . .'

'But the argument is irrefutable. My golly. This chap certainly read the play carefully. Listen. It says that the Jews are the rightful heirs to Palestine because they are descended from Abraham through his real son Isaac, while the Arabs are only descended from the slave-son Ishmael. But now the British are trying to make the point—very subtly, of course, but we know how subtle British diplomacy is—that the Arabs are the true heirs because they are descended from *Esau*, who was older than his brother Jacob, and was swindled out of his older-brother rights.'

'And that's all in the play?'

'Of course. The two characters in the play are Algernon Moncrieff, who lives in a flat in London, and Jack Worthing, who lives in the country. Well, aren't they the exact characters as described in the Bible? Jacob is described in the Bible as *'a quiet man, dwelling in tents'*—that's obviously Moncrieff in his flat, and Esau is *'a cunning hunter, a man of the field'*—obviously

Worthing, living in the country. They start off as having no connection, and then discover that they are brothers. But who is the *older* brother? It's Worthing, who is really Esau. It says here that Lady Bracknell says explicitly in Act III: "Worthing is the older brother." Does she?'

'She certainly does.'

'Well there you are. This is how he ends: "This play must be stopped, with all its disgraceful twisting of history".'

'It's stopped all right,' Briscombe said morosely. 'I suppose I should have put on *Peter Pan*—or is that too political?'

I commiserated with him: he commiserated with me. We emerged somewhat unsteadily from the cool shade of the restaurant into the sunny world around us, and struggled towards the Damascus Gate, where we took leave of each other. If Briscombe was in a cheerful mood by now he was still in full possession of his wits, and as we parted he spoke of something casually, but seriously, that he had obviously kept for this moment.

'I want to pass on something from Hardcastle,' he said. 'I think you should know.'

'Hardcastle gave you a message for me?'

'No, he didn't. But he talked about you. He's not an ordinary policeman, you know: he's on special C.I.D. duty in connection with illegal immigration, arms-running and all that. He mentioned to me—not officially—that you seemed to have some special connection with a man they have their eye on, a chap called Shapiro. He doesn't think you're in with him necessarily, but he has to watch these things. He asked about you and I said that if Shapiro really was involved in any of these things I was sure you didn't know. But I decided to tell you. I think he really wanted me to slip you a word.'

I laughed. 'Oh dear. I must obviously watch out. Very good of you to warn me. I must say, Shapiro has been very nice to me. Do you think he would know that they have their eye on him?'

'I imagine he might guess. For all I know he may be deliberately drawing attention to himself to take attention off others. One can never tell. It's all a bit mixed up here. I don't think we're entirely whole-hearted in the Government about what we interfere with. We like to know what's going on, but sometimes we turn a blind eye on things.'

'Such as the underground defence movement—*Haganah*?'

'Yes. It's an open secret that the Jews have organized themselves for defence. They have to, especially in the outlying settlements, and even in settled places it's useful for the Arabs to know that they wouldn't get away with some campaign of violence. A thing like that could blow up suddenly without rhyme or reason—like the massacre of those harmless old Jews in Hebron in 1929. Naturally we have to crack down from time to time, but we've never gone all out to destroy, or even interfere with the Haganah. Just watch it.'

'One of Hardcastle's jobs?'

'Yes, he's pretty good at it. Did something similar in Nigeria. There's only one snag here. It's easy for the British to keep a guiding hand on the natives. We could handle the Arabs all right. But it's the Jews, isn't it?'

'I suppose it is.'

'They just won't behave like natives, will they? And yet this is supposed to be their native land. Quite a problem.'

'Quite.'

* * *

If I tried to describe the most important thing that happened in the next few weeks I might say—perhaps for a paradox—that it was my recalling the picture of Malcah holding the old coin—the *pruta*—in her hand. Everything else that went on round me in Jerusalem was predictable—even how it all had to end. But remembering Malcah and the coin suggested something to me one day when I was up at the University listening to a lecture. A coin was such a clear thing—something firm to start with. The thought seemed to start climbing into my mind and then fall back again. But when it emerged later, it proved quite important to me.

In the meantime everything else went on as expected, even if

JERUSALEM

the predictable for Jerusalem might have seemed startling elsewhere. Shapiro asked me to his house to meet his wife, a warm, comfortable-looking woman. Neither of them said anything about the home they supported for orphan girls, but Shapiro, talking to me alone in his sitting-room after supper, while his wife washed the dishes, broached a subject not entirely unconnected. He was still anxious for me to become the formal British head of his projected agency in England, or if not, at least to put him in touch with someone who would, which sounded more possible. But it would be so much better, he argued, if I did it myself because this would make it possible for me to come regularly on visits to Palestine—and perhaps even more, as he then proceeded to explain. He had a proposition for me. It would cost me nothing. I could even earn a fee if I wanted it, but it would be a good deed in itself. It would save a life. Would I marry a refugee girl in Germany and bring her to Palestine on my British passport? There was no need to get involved personally with the girl if I didn't want to. Divorce for Jews in Palestine was the easiest thing in the world—little more than a statement of intent before a rabbi, or indeed any witnesses. On the other hand, one of the girls he had in mind was a delightful creature—an orphan, desperate to come to Palestine but with no immediate chance. In any case, by getting her in this way it would leave a place in the queue for someone less fortunate.

'But really . . .' I began to splutter.

'Now don't get excited,' Shapiro said. 'Maybe it's a surprise. But that's what's wrong with you. You've lived a sheltered life in England. You're so innocent. Grow up a little. Let me ask you. You like women, I daresay. And you're not married, or engaged to be married. All right. What are you waiting for? You're waiting, I suppose, to fall madly in love with somebody who will at the same moment fall madly in love with you. Don't you think that's going to be quite a coincidence?'

He seemed to have got me into a corner somehow. 'I suppose it is a bit unlikely,' I admitted sheepishly.

'*Unlikely*! That's a mild word for it. It's all right as a game, but why should you assume that the Ribbono Shel Olam likes playing games? The British like games: they're brought up that way. Everything has to be played according to the rules of cricket. I saw it when I lived in England. It's fine if the whole world was England, but it isn't. I tell you: I have a strong suspicion that the Ribbono Shel Olam doesn't play cricket. He doesn't even like to *watch* cricket. Life isn't a game. Life is something—what shall I say?—life is something to be lived through. A game is when you can count on everybody accepting the same rules as you do. Well, is that what happens in the world? Look at Hitler! Look at the Arabs! Are they playing according to the rules? Should one just stand there at the—what do you call it—the stump. . . .'

'The wicket.'

'That's it. The wicket. Should one just stand there patiently at the wicket and let them throw a bomb at you instead of a cricket ball? It doesn't make sense really, does it?'

'No, it doesn't. But in ordinary relations between human beings. . . .'

'Same thing exactly. As long as you don't expect everything to fit into your own rules you can get along. Perhaps life is learning to live with the unexpected. Now take tonight. I've thrown a bomb at you—well, let's say a hand-grenade. You're going through life waiting for something wonderful to happen, like in a fairy-story for children, and I'm suggesting to you that maybe you can behave like an adult and take charge of your own life—and do some good at the same time. But you're too shocked. All right. You've got over the shock now. Is my proposal so extraordinary? Don't you agree that if you could help someone—some young girl—to escape to a free life here it would be worth doing? Have you never heard of anyone coming in on a married visa this way, just by an agreed arrangement to get two people in instead of only one?'

I had indeed heard of it. I thought of Malcah in Florence explaining in a matter of fact way that she was doing just that. But this had been about somebody else, not *me*.

'Take Palestine itself,' he went on. 'You're looking at it from the outside. You come on a visit, and you'll go back. You just haven't opened your mind to the idea of getting involved here, have you? And yet if you weren't just playing cricket, you could do a lot just because you happen to have a British passport. You could come in here to live for a while—bringing a German girl with you—but keep your British nationality so that we could run the agency in England under your name. That's what I would call making the most of a situation. As a matter of fact, if you divorced the girl, you could do it a second time—and a third time....'

'Oh really, Yitzchak! You want me to be a Bluebeard.'

'And why not? As long as you don't actually kill the girls. A Bluebeard who made the girls happy by setting them free, what's wrong with that?'

'I don't think I can plan things that way.'

'No, my friend, I think that's your trouble. You'd rather let things just happen to you, wouldn't you? Well,' he smiled, 'there are so many ways of living. Who's to say what is the right way? But there's just one thing, a word of warning. Can I give it to you?'

'Please do.'

'If you insist on just standing there peacefully at the stump—the wicket, I mean—don't be surprised if the cricket-ball explodes in your face one day. That's really the only kind of cricket that the Ribbono Shel Olam plays, you know. It can happen to you. It can happen to England, too. Do you see what I mean?'

'I'm beginning to.'

He looked at me sharply, but with a certain affection. 'Yes, I think you are. But you would still rather find an old Hebrew manuscript, wouldn't you? Something sensational. *Your* discovery. Well, I suppose I'll have to help you.'

'No news from your cousin Hermann?'

'Oh no, I've had no time for that yet. Everything takes time, especially when you're dealing with Arabs. But if this is really what you want to take back from Palestine, we'll find something for you. Listen, does it have to be 2,000 years old? Maybe not quite so old will also be interesting. The only important thing for you is that it shouldn't be about the world of today, the real world. Isn't that right?'

There I was, backed into a corner again.

★ ★ ★

But it seemed quite different when I told Yael about it. We had been talking one day about the kind of work that really brought satisfaction. I had read her a chapter of my book, which I had finally got down to; and when I went on to talk about the possibility of finding something myself—something tangible to put the subject in different focus—her eyes lit up with immediate interest.

I was seeing a good deal of her, not regularly, but when she seemed to need me. She was away a lot from Jerusalem, sometimes with her husband, who spent many days away at his various stations, and sometimes, I gathered, by herself. Even when she was in Jerusalem, days would pass when we wouldn't meet. She might say she was working, or not bother with any explanation. But then without notice she would be at my door some bright morning; or if I telephoned her home, as I sometimes did, consumed by a sudden longing to hear her voice, she would ask me to drop in at her studio that afternoon or on the next afternoon.

I would sit there watching her at work. Wherever she stood, her dark beauty fused into the colour and texture of the world around her and merged with the world outside. It was a tangible miracle to me; and behind the ease and laughter I saw the relief she felt to be with me, as if I were some kind of shelter for her. In the intervals I went on with my work, saw many other people, visited her and her husband sometimes for a quiet evening or a party—it was as if I was satisfied to be the comfortable person she had liked from the beginning. This was the role she has assigned to me. I was too happy to try and change it.

I had been trying to find out discreetly at the University if there was any interest among the experts in finding things in

JERUSALEM

caves, but the feeling seemed to be that this was not a fruitful line. It was true that the dry air in a sealed cave could keep things in good condition for a long period, but it was more likely that the great discoveries that everybody hoped for would be made by normal excavation, as at Lachish.

My idea had therefore retreated from reality. I had been down to the Dead Sea once for the day with Briscombe when he had visited Jericho on official business, but I had not sought out cousin Hermann, feeling that this was something that had to come through Shapiro.

I told Yael all this while she stood working at her sculpture, and the story of Hermann and his Bedouin rumours seemed to start a train of thought in her mind. 'It would be useful if you could pin him down,' she said, 'but in any case I have an idea. Would you like to go down there for a few days with me? We could go down and do some climbing ourselves in the hills around the Dead Sea?'

'Just the two of us?'

'No, that wouldn't be wise, or even very useful. We would need some people with us who knew the country well and could speak Arabic like natives. I could arrange something, though. Let me think about it.'

I was more than happy that she should care so much. It was at a time when I had been seeing rather less of her. She seemed, somehow, preoccupied. A few days passed; but one morning when I telephoned she sounded cheerful again and had a wonderful idea, not about the Dead Sea but for what could almost be a rehearsal. 'It's such a lovely day,' she said. 'I feel stifled—I would love to get out into the country. If you are free, we could take the car and drive to Ain Harif. It's an Arab village about twelve miles to the west, near the ruins of a Crusader Castle. There are only a few ruins of the Castle left, but it would make a good target for a picnic.'

It proved in fact just as wonderful as it sounded. The village—it was really a small town—was apparently holding its market day. There were throngs of Arabs of every colour and garb crowded round the stalls and shops, and shouting in the open square at some kind of sale of camels that was proceeding. Perhaps it wasn't a sale but a dispute over ownership. I couldn't decide. The crowd was partly due, as we could see, to a session being held in a dingy building which proved to be the District Court. There were a few stray policemen standing around the Court door, with Arabs—plaintiffs, witnesses, or just onlookers—squatting patiently outside in the sunshine.

Of the Castle, high up on the hill overlooking (and once guarding) the village, little was left except a massive old wall showing remnants of fretted tracery and a stone frieze; but the setting alone was enough. The site had obviously been selected to dominate the road from Jerusalem to the coast. High up on the hill, great masses of rock must have been hacked out by thousands of workmen—Crusaders or natives—so that the masonry of the Castle had become part of the mountain itself, with an eagle's view from its parapet. All was silent now amid the ruins. We sat in the shadow of the wall, eating our sandwiches and drinking wine.

I had been burbling with talk about the Crusades, full of a book I had read; and Yael, leaning back against the rock, her eyes half-closed, was looking at me with some of her usual amusement.

'You really like the Crusaders, don't you?' she said. 'You've adopted them as your ancestors.'

I was lying stretched out at full length on the ground, basking happily in the sun. 'My ancestors?' I said. 'I don't know. I suppose one just plays this game if one is brought up in England It's such a marvellous period of history—unbelievable really. I suppose I find it exciting: the thought of those Englishmen and Frenchmen coming here a thousand years ago and building all this, just driven by an idea. . . .'

'How many Jews did they massacre on the way?' she asked. 'All the way through Germany and France and Italy—and of course when they finally captured Jerusalem—every adult Jew put to the sword. . . .'

'Ah yes,' I said slowly. 'The massacre in Jerusalem. *Your* ancestors, I suppose. . . .'

'I suppose so. In my childhood there were still stories—Aleppo, Antioch, and Jerusalem. . . .'

I was trying to work something out. 'It's very odd,' I said. 'I feel entirely at home with the ancient rabbis—of the time of the Midrash—and then there's a huge gap and my grandfather appears on the scene in Russia. I've no idea where I was in between. Of course I know the history of it, but me personally—yes, I've had to adopt my ancestors, even the Crusaders. I know one thing. When I was a boy I was completely on their side when they were fighting Saladin.'

She laughed. 'Then you must have been very unhappy, because you lost.'

'I was. Terribly.'

'I was on the other side,' she said. 'One of my ancestors was a doctor with Saladin, according to our family tradition. We claim descent from Samuel Ibn Albarkala of Damascus. . . . And yet I know so little about it really—just my mother told me about our family, and her father had told her—and his father—and so on.'

'I wonder if it's so very different,' I said. 'They're quite real to you, but then the things I feel are very real to me, too. I have such a vivid picture of it all. Up there in the rock, an isolated Crusader Court, half French, half Oriental, the men in suits of mail and Arab headdress—golden kafiyehs set with precious stones—the large Cross on their shields, the chivalry and the brutality, the huge feasts and the years of austerity in between—it's part of all our history, isn't it?—the watchmen in armour up there on the tower, the great clang of the portcullis when they spy Saladin's horsemen. . . . I can even see your great-great-grandfather the doctor, riding along with his little black bag—'

'Giving Saladin an aspirin, I suppose.'

'No, no—a love potion. I'm sure he could concoct the most wonderful love potions. . . .'

She stretched out her hand lazily and took mine. 'We've finally found a meeting-point,' she said. 'Yes, let's agree on the love potion.'

I looked up into her smiling eyes. 'Have you ever had a love potion' I asked her.

'Do you think I need one?'

'No, I wouldn't have thought so; but here in the East there must be so much remembered magic——'

'Yes, there is magic. Perhaps I've drunk the love potion without knowing it.' She still held my hand, but her eyes were far away now.

I moved up to where I could sit beside her. 'I have an idea,' I said. 'Let's find the Witch of Endor and get her to mix a love potion for both of us to drink.'

'Perhaps she could mix a happiness potion instead.'

'Instead? Isn't love something to make one happy?'

'Do you think it is? Yes, perhaps one kind of love makes one happy. The feeling I have for you makes me happy. But that's because there's happiness in you.'

'And in you?'

'Don't ask me questions I can't answer,' she said. 'I am happy at this moment. And now, just when I'm happy, we have to go.' She lifted both hands up to be helped to her feet. We gathered up our things and got ready to go.

Coming back through the village, we saw that the crowd had thinned a good deal, and we stopped for a while to take a coffee from a little booth in the square. I suggested to Yael that it might be fun to see if the Court was still in session, and at that moment, looking over to the door of the squat little building, we saw a familiar tall lean figure emerge—Inspector Hardcastle, in uniform. We waved and he came over to chat, cursing good-humouredly at the fantastic lying of the Arab witnesses in the case he had been attending. He groaned with envy when I told him about our picnic at the Castle, lamenting urgent business in Jaffa that would force him to drive there now without even a chance to spend some time looking at the ruins. He went off to get his car, and soon we saw it emerge from behind the Courthouse, a big black open Lancia, which shot by us with a roar towards the west. I assumed from his friendliness towards me that Briscombe's reassurances had been enough to stifle any suspicions he had about my bona fides; but I wondered vaguely if Shapiro's activities had moved across the line in a way that might now lead to action against him. I hoped not.

★ ★ ★

Again some days passed without my seeing Yael. It was getting hotter as Easter—and Passover—approached, but it was the sense of political thunder in the air which riveted one's attention. Surely with all the black headlines and screaming editorials, the endless meetings and arguments, the bitter internal quarrels within each community—the wild accusations, the struggle for power—surely it would come to breaking point. Was there a sign in the increase of 'incidents' that one read of—some shooting in outlying places, attacks and thieving that might be local or might mean something else? No one was sure. The days were long and sunny. The rains had gone: the spring flowers everywhere were wild with colour. Perhaps the passion in the landscape demanded some echo. In the Old City itself the sap of fervour rose every year at this time with the endless religious processions that were themselves almost riots of passion: Ramadan had just gone by with its fanatical celebrations; the Christian pilgrims were assembling from far and near, with every kind of sect fighting fiercely for its rights; the Jews, as always, were beating their breasts at the Wailing Wall. Even the British had caught some of the excitement. The *Palestine Post* carried daily bulletins from London on the Boat Race, due the following week, and the betting among the British was wild, with Cambridge heavily favoured. Spring was in the air too at the St George's Sports Ground, where cricket bats were being carefully oiled in preparation for the match against the Haifa Harlequins.

Sirov's name was in the papers a good deal, I saw, because of the increasing urgency of his call for unity with the Arabs. But though what he said on this always came out with great force, in conversation at home he was as gentle and courteous as ever, wryly humorous about persons and politics, sceptical about most things, loving to Yael, attentive to his guests. I had been invited well in advance to the large party they always gave for the Seder on the first night of Passover, and I wondered if there would be Arabs this time among the guests. I was sure there would be Christians. We had always had some Christian guests even at my father's Seder.

It was just about ten days before the Seder that Yael dropped in at my flat one morning with news. She was in a gay mood, and my room, littered with books and papers, seemed to come to life with her sparkle.

'I've arranged it,' she said. 'Your Dead Sea expedition. Your great discovery can now be made!'

'Oh, wonderful!' I said. 'When can we go? Who's coming with us?'

'Two young men from Alex's plant station near Tel Aviv,' she said. 'I wanted them to come because they're just the right two, so I waited till they could get leave. I know you'll like them: Josef and Meir. They both speak Arabic fluently. Josef is a sabra, and has a good knowledge of archaeology, by the way. He's very keen on it. Meir's been here since he was a child. Of course they know a lot about plants too. We can live off the land if we get lost!'

'Could we persuade them to lose *us*?'

'Now really. I thought you were serious. Don't you want to make a great discovery? The caves? The manuscripts? Or do you only want a rendezvous with me?'

'Can I choose?'

'Oh, I see. English humour. But seriously, aren't you pleased?'

'I'm delighted. But there's just one thing. I've given up hope.'

'Of finding anything?'

'The more I've talked here to the people who know, the less likely it seems that anything could be found, even by an expert. I met a German professor the other day at the University who proved to me by all the laws of chemistry that no parchment could possibly survive from Bible times. And as for the caves, they've all been explored.'

'So you don't want to go?'

JERUSALEM

'Of course I want to go. I'm dying to go. When do we leave?'
'On Monday.'
'Before Pesach?'
'We can have four good days. I don't have to get back before Thursday night for the Seder on Friday.'
'What about your Seder party?'
'Oh, my cook will arrange all that. She always prefers to do all the shopping and arranging by herself. Have you met her? Frau Apfel. Very dominating. I have to keep out of her way.'
'Well, that's fine. So we're off to the wilderness. What do I have to take with me besides a jug of wine, a loaf of bread, and thou?'
'You're really not very serious, are you?'
'I'm terribly serious. But having you here in the room with me makes me cheerful.'

She looked at me and said nothing for a moment. Then she came across to and kissed me softly. 'You haven't changed,' she said. 'I'm so glad.' Then she broke off. 'Yes, let's be practical. All you need is some strong boots and a rucksack, and some blankets—or better still a sleeping bag. I'm sure you don't have one. But I can get Josef to bring you one. He can bring you a rucksack, too. I thought we wouldn't make any special plans, but work things out with Josef and Meir when we get down there and they begin asking the Arabs questions. We could spend a night or two at one of the monasteries—there are a few down there in isolated places. Or we could sleep in the open if the weather is good. The main thing is to walk and climb. And you will see the wilderness in spring—in many places it blooms like a garden with wild flowers. . . .'

A faint flicker of doubt had crossed my mind when she spoke of going away so close to the Seder, but I was too happy to want to raise any questions; and on Monday morning at eight a large rough-looking car was at my door with a tall, dark-skinned young man smiling at the wheel, and his companion, equally young and sunburned, but more rotund in figure, leaping out to hand me a rucksack that bulged with a sleeping-bag. We proved too early for Yael when we went round to pick her up. She was busy with her staff and preoccupied on the telephone for more than an hour; but in due course we were all ready and on our way out of Jerusalem, winding our way down towards Jericho.

The two young men were in front. I sat in the back with Yael, touching her hand lightly and happy to be with her. The road was familiar, but no familiarity could ever soften the writhing agony of that seared volcanic landscape as we began to drop down towards the cleft of the Jordan. Within a few minutes, it seemed, all fertility and life had been wiped out. The arid rocks, glowing blood-red or gashed with black ravines, brought into one's mind every savage story of their history—the evil of Sodom and Gomorrah, the pitiless slaughters by the conquering Israelites under Joshua, the last desperate resistance to the Romans at Massada. Already as we descended into the valley, the heat clung like a blanket. To the left of the winding road the deep dark gorge of the Wadi el-Kelt fell away, with a glimpse of water six hundred feet below. To the right, hung high in the precipice, was a grim-looking monastery, a kind of penitentiary, I was told, for unruly or criminal monks. The road wound on and then, suddenly, there was the view of the Jordan plain, the green fertile triangle surrounded by the desert, the darker green ribbon of water winding through it, the purple mountains of Moab flung into the sky as a backcloth to the deep blue of the Dead Sea.

It was close to noon. We ate something light in Jericho and the two young men disappeared for a while to see if there might be any news to pick up from wandering Bedouin or other gossip-vendors. Yael and I walked round the dreary sun-baked town for a while. There was nothing left to see of the stately city that Herod and Cleopatra had known—a kind of Nice, full of luxurious villas, theatres and palaces. Today all this had blown away, and Jericho was more like something out of a Western movie—a little frontier town, as it had been originally when Joshua's trumpets had shaken down its dusty adobe walls. There were soldiers and police wandering about in assorted uniforms, a few dismal Government buildings, a bank office, a mixture of de-

JERUSALEM

sultory traffic—lorries loaded with Dead Sea chemicals, camels and donkeys with less obvious burdens—something smuggled, one expected, from across the Jordan. One thing had not changed over the ages—the unbearably languid heat at a thousand feet below sea-level, and the bewildering tropical fertility it produced with figs, bananas, bamboos, dates and the heavy scent of oranges and balsam. And there was another feeling, too, that had survived—that it was the crossing point to something mysteriously exciting on the other side—Gilead, where the rich Greek city-states had left ruins of legendary beauty, a constant hint to the Jews of the wealth that had existed once and could grow again. As Yael and I stood outside the little hotel, a bus swung in, loaded with thirty or forty cheerful Jewish schoolchildren, who got out when the bus stopped to stretch their legs. Brown, round and happy in their short skin-tight trousers and blue blouses, they were like an injection of energy into the indolence around us. They had been on a trip to Transjordan to visit Petra, in the south, as part of the intensive touring and hiking that so many of the young people did at this time of the year. 'You should go there, too,' Yael said to me. 'And to Jerash. It has such a different atmosphere from Palestine.'

But after a while the sight and sound of so much chattering energy exhausted us, and we went inside to wait in the shade. There was a great lassitude in the air. I was sitting dozing in a chair in a corner, so sleepy that when I saw the young men return and go over to Yael for what seemed like a quiet but rapid-fire conversation, I thought vaguely that I would wait until they had told me the outcome. They seemed in no hurry to look for me, and sitting there with eyes half closed, I began to get the feeling that their conversation with Yael was somehow too intense to be related to the planning of our leisurely reconnaissance, unless, of course, they had discovered something sensational. I was rousing myself when I saw the young men go off hurriedly, almost as if they had agreed on something important that now had to be done. Yael then turned to look for me and came over smilingly to explain what had happened. They had come across some story, she said, that they thought best to follow up alone. We would leave them for the rest of the day and start our walk the next morning, depending on what they found out. Why shouldn't we two go down to the Dead Sea that afternoon ourselves for a quiet swim and a drink? We could at the same time try and find out what Hermann could tell us.

I was a little surprised at the delay in starting, but there was nothing pleasanter that I could have wanted. Thoughts of a dusty strenuous climb starting in the heat of the day were distinctly less attractive. Within no time at all, Yael and I had taken the car and were on our way down to the little bathing-beach at Kallia. In duty bound, we first looked for Hermann. He was in Jerusalem, we were told. There was obviously a curse on meeting Hermann; but the sea was there, and we were soon bouncing round on its sticky surface. Sipping our long gin-slaked orange drinks later under a striped umbrella, cool and relaxed after a fresh-water shower, we agreed laughingly that this was a much better way of spending a hot afternoon. Yael was looking at me in her old way, slightly from a distance but with great tenderness. I was still a comfortable person to have around in times of trouble. But that was just it: in times of trouble. There was something odd going on that I hadn't fathomed.

There were only two vacant rooms at the Jericho hotel, both very scruffy. Yael had the smaller one, and I had the only bed in the other, with the two young men due to sleep on the floor when they returned. They had not got back by the time Yael, yawning freely from the swim and the general lassitude, announced that she was retiring. I assumed that Josef and Meir must have slipped across to Transjordan to pursue some story. They were still out when I too went to bed. When I woke up in the morning, uncomfortable in the heat, their sleeping bags were stretched out but they, it seemed, were up already—obviously fiends of energy. I got up, and seeing no sign of Yael went out for a little stroll before breakfast. When I got back I saw Josef and Meir seated together in the little coffee-room and caught sight of Yael standing at a primitive wall-telephone in the owner's sitting-room. She saw me too and waved cheerfully.

I went across to greet my room-mates, and found them full of good tidings.

'We've got something quite interesting,' Josef said. 'We were down at the excavations talking to the Arabs working there, and they say we're not the first to ask. A couple of months ago some Bedouin were in Jericho with some story about old pots and writings they found in a cave—very secretive. We tried to find out where these Bedouin might be now. We followed some story that they were across there'—he waved towards the Jordan—'but it didn't work. Someone said he'd heard they had intended to go south, to En-Gedi—I expect you know it well enough from the Bible.'

'Where David found Saul in a cave *covering his feet?*'

'That's one cave we will avoid,' said Meir jocularly.

'From what we heard,' Josef said, 'it sounded as if these rumours began after they had been camping for a while nearer the *northern* end of the Dead Sea. En-Gedi is about twenty miles south. We could try either, really.'

'I wish we could have a bit of a climb today,' I said. 'I feel in the mood. It seems much cooler.'

'Yes, it's cooler. A good walk and a climb would be good. I think we could plan something.'

At that point Yael came over. 'You've heard the news,' she said to me. 'Good news for you, but bad news for me. I've just been telephoning my home. Frau Apfel is ill. I think I'll just have to go back. Without her, nothing will be ordered for the Seder. You three will have to go on alone.'

She saw my disappointment, and tried to cheer me up. 'You men are much better off without a woman to hold you back, aren't you? What are you planning to do, Josef?'

'I thought we'd work our way round Nebi Musah towards El Mintar,' he said. 'There are always a lot of Bedouin camped on the slopes between there and the Wadi Qumran. Once we get up to El Mintar and Bir-es Suk, we can get a really good view.' He had pulled out a map. 'You can see the old names on this,' he said to me. 'We would be looking down into the Wad en Nar. That's the Brook Kidron in the Bible.'

'Oh, I'd like to see that. Ezekial's torrent that will swarm with fish.'

'No sign of fish yet,' Joseph said. 'Not all prophecies come true. Some do,' he added quietly, 'but not all. But we will get a view up there, all the way south of the Wadi Qumran towards Ain Feshkhah, and there are many caves we can look at. You'll get an idea of the feel of the mountains and the wilderness. I think that if you're writing about that period it should help.'

'Don't expect to find anything,' Meir said, still jocular. 'You know the Arabs. They like to make up stories.'

'Well, you may not find any new caves,' Josef said, 'and you certainly won't find any fish. But you may find something else.'

'Such as?' I asked.

'Oh, I don't know. There's something about wandering in the wilderness. It gives one ideas. I know: I've done a lot of it. Well, we all have, haven't we? Forty years of it.'

* * *

It was all cheerful except for Yael's sudden decision to leave. This was peculiar. Something was going on. I felt it most when we turned and waved good-bye to her. But it all faded once we were out on foot among the crags and precipices. For the first few hours it had been an easy walk, but soon we were climbing —or scrambling—along sheep and goat tracks, or along the rock itself, picking our way according to the map from point to point. It was not the kind of walk, I thought, that Heather had had in mind—the Pilgrim's Way to Canterbury. This was a little rougher. We had left the main Jerusalem to Jericho road far to the north, but we crossed a couple of other well-worn tracks along which occasional caravans of camels and Arabs wound their slow way—perhaps still carrying the balm of Gilead and the salt of the Dead Sea that their ancestors had carried along these tracks immemorially. When we met some Arabs Josef and Meir moved among them confidently, talking, laughing, with the greatest friendliness. They seemed to explain that I was a distinguished visitor from England, which led to some florid phrase-making and much touching of the forehead. On the lower slopes too we met some shepherd boys whom they spoke to, but then we left the world behind, puffing our way to the top of the first really steep crag that lay ahead.

Looking round from the peak, the view seemed limitless. One could imagine Mt Hermon, far to the north, snowy father of all the hills we saw as the northern background, framing the rich plains of Jordan. To the east always was the deep blue lake, glowing in the sun like a burnished mirror. Moving on along the plateau we came to a point where, by a freak of the fantastic twisting of rock that lay below, we caught a glimpse of a new road—narrow but with a good enough surface for cars—that led down to the Dead Sea. A number of lorries were moving along it; then a caravan passed by—all in utter silence, though the clear air brought the picture to us in absolute detail. A big black car—only a dot, but a clear *concept* of a fast car—sped by down the road, reminding me automatically of Inspector Hardcastle hurtling off with a deep roar in his Lancia from Ain Harif. It brought back to my mind the joy of that picnic in the shadow of the Crusader Castle, and I sighed to think that the magic of those hours with Yael had somehow receded. There was something else in the air now. I thought of Shapiro laughing at my innocence in expecting love to be something miraculous—a *coup de foudre* that struck two people simultaneously. Wasn't it rather that paths crossed, with each of us still surrounded by a personal wilderness?

Was I not still alone, even with the thought of her beauty moving me, and the feeling of how she turned to me for the warmth I gave her? And how easy it was to see here among these bare rocks the things that so disturbed her, the torment of life that drove her as fiercely as Yael in the Bible, who saw Sisera lying at her feet and stretched out her hand for the hammer....

She had only gentleness for me, but the fierceness of these rocks was inside her, as fierce as the Hebrew of Deborah's Song. It was different for Heather on the Pilgrim's Way to Canterbury, with the soft green fields stretching peacefully towards quiet churches and cheerful hostelries. There was no such peace here, with the enemy Sisera to be trapped and the whole of life tautened to the pitch of violence—

> *She put her hand to the nail and her right hand to the workmen's hammer,*
> *And with the hammer she smote Sisera.* . . .

I murmured the words of the Song nostalgically to myself, and suddenly found to my surprise that I was smiling at my own idiocy. How readily I turned away from myself to some ancient story. When would I stop taking refuge behind all these bugbears of my infancy? On the day I stopped being an infant, presumably. Well, it was at least an encouraging sign if I could recognize it. Was this the message of the wilderness? Other people before me had had other messages: they came out into the wilderness to find God. But this was a bit hard for me: I had a feeling that God had made the decision on this already. Lots of people tried to find God, but not everybody had the talent. Perhaps God preferred it that way—as in the classic theatrical agent's phrase: 'Don't call *us*: we'll call *you*.' That was how it always worked in the Bible: *And the word of the Lord came unto Amos.* . . . Well then: if I wasn't going to find God, what *would* I find out here? Again there was a cliché waiting: 'myself'. But I had an intuition about this. I could learn to be alone out here, or anywhere. There was an immense satisfaction in being alone: it was safe—unassailable. But it was not me: it was only half of me. The other half was what I gave and received. What the wilderness seemed to be saying was: the world is not a wilderness.

Far from being sad and mystical, I felt happy out here—happy at the thought of Yael and her beauty—happy to have found her—happy even to recognize, as I did so clearly, that there was nothing easy or ordered about it all. I was simply glad to be alive—and I was hungry. I turned towards Josef and Meir, feeling almost like Elijah in the wilderness looking up for the ravens to feed him. The days of miracles were of course over, but lo—as the Bible says—it happened. Out of the capacious rucksacks came great hunks of bread and sausage, with a flask of fresh water that tasted like wine. And here was I doubting the wisdom of the Bible. Had any Biblical story been more fulfilled? *'And he went and dwelt by the Brook Cherith that was before Jordan, and the ravens brought him bread and flesh in the morning and bread and flesh in the evening and he drank of the brook. . . .'*

'Are we anywhere near the Brook Cherith?' I asked Josef. 'It was supposed to be near the Jordan.'

'You mean Elijah and the ravens? It's never been found. Every name in the Bible practically has been identified, except for that.'

Meir chipped in with his mouth full. 'Elijah must have made the whole thing up.'

'Oh dear,' I said, 'and I had just decided that the Bible was true. My last prop is gone. Ah well, I suppose we'd better move on. Which way now?'

'Do you really feel like passing a night in the open—in the wilderness?' Josef asked.

'As long as the ravens come to feed me in the evening.'

'Oh yes, we have plenty to eat. Let me tell you what we had in mind. We thought of exploring an old route that we think once existed from Ain el Trabeh on the Dead Sea—about nine or ten miles below Ain Feshkhah—direct across the hills towards Hebron. That's the Wilderness of Tekoa, of course.'

'Wasn't the main route further south, from En-Gedi?'

'Yes, that's a familiar way in the Bible, either down to Hebron or up to Jerusalem. But if there really is this intermediate path, it might be interesting. We could work straight across now towards the hill of Tekoa itself and perhaps spend the night there.'

'With the ghost of Amos, I suppose. Are there still shepherds up there? It must be a pretty rough place to have made him so vitriolic in his prophecies.'

'He just hated town folk, the way all country folk do. Yes, there are stray shepherds up there. We'll talk to them. These rumours of caves may begin to add up. And then we can work our way down towards the Dead Sea and back to Jericho.'

And so two blissful days followed, lost to the world of town life and politics. We walked, sometimes at a good pace, sometimes lingering while Josef pointed out historical places, or plants and flowers mentioned in the Bible. We scrambled sometimes up the bare slopes: we talked to wandering shepherds or to Arabs in the odd half-hidden camps that we came across up little gullies or down in the plain. At night, after a staggering sunset, the stars came down magically and the bright moon—almost the full moon of Passover—silvered the crags around us. Josef and Meir were perfectly matched in temper, the one quiet and commanding, the other rotund and jocular. I noticed that they were most skilful with compass and map, and that they made notes sometimes after talking to the Arabs we met. It was almost as if they were on a military reconnaissance, like the twelve men, one from each tribe, whom Moses sent out in the Book of Numbers to spy out the land....

And suddenly, as the thought came to me, I realized exactly what the whole journey was about. Two young men, with perfect Arabic, wandering round innocently with an English visitor, picking up the rumours in the Jericho market-place and among the stray Bedouin, looking into alternative routes along which soldiers might have marched and could march again—wasn't it all obvious? Whether it was *Haganah* or some other form of defence, military preparation in a land like this meant more than barrack-square drill or shooting practice. It meant constant training walks out in the wilds—endless reconnaissance, with one eye cocked for trouble. And Yael? Her peculiarly energetic bearing, her odd absences from Jerusalem—there was something here too, even if I couldn't put my finger on it. Of course we would still be asking about caves and other discoveries. This was no pretence. They were as keen on archaeology as on defending their ancient land. It was one and the same thing.

How tactful not to have involved me directly by an explanation of what they were up to. I looked up at my two spies with renewed affection. *Two* spies! Of course. These were not Moses' twelve, but the two spies whom Joshua had sent in to

JERUSALEM

Jericho and who had been given such friendly protection from the police by Rahab the Harlot. I had always liked that story, the undoubted progenitor of all the hundreds which had followed in literature of tough women with a heart of gold. Yes, it was a nice story, but one I didn't care to pursue at the moment.

★ ★ ★

It was Wednesday afternoon and we were on our way down towards the Dead Sea when the real character of our little journey had come into my head. Josef had changed his original idea to come out at Ain el Trabeh, having picked up an apparently strong rumour which hinted at some interesting caves in the hills just north of Ain el Ghuweir. There was a high ridge there near Tubk Amriyeh, where the Kidron made a final tortured descent into the sea, about five miles south of the Wadi Qumran. It was worth trying, and we were in good spirits. Josef and Meir seemed satisfied with what they had learnt about the old tracks they had been looking for. On my side I was pleased enough to think that the stories pointed at last to somewhere specific, since all our other cave explorations had led to nothing. If some old things had actually been rummaged out of caves here, others nearby might be equally productive.

I had no illusions about walking into a cave and picking a manuscript up off the floor. Josef had made it clear to me that all we could hope for was to verify that the area had yielded something. If by chance we came across a cave hitherto sealed up, the floor would be covered deep with the debris and filth of thousands of years. One would need a whole team of workers to dig the stuff out—and then it would be bits of parchment mixed up with animal skins and bone and hair and slime. There really was not much to hope for.

By three o'clock we had arrived roughly in the area selected and had begun to scramble up the steep ridges, among the contorted strata of limestone and flint, littered sometimes with bush and shingle. The heat beat down on us. Sometimes there were openings in the rocks which were at least a brief shelter, even if they were not caves. In other places great boulders stood in our way, perhaps dropped there in some volcanic surge, or perhaps rolled there by human hands to seal up a cave. One would never know. We met an occasional wild goat, staring down disdainfully from a crag, and once we saw a boy chasing one of his family's sheep. Josef spoke to him and decided to move a little more inland. It was all hot, exhausting, and fruitless. Behind us the Dead Sea was a calm enigmatic reminder of man's propensity to give himself a lot of trouble for no good reason. At about five we gave up and decided to make our way back somehow to Jericho.

We wound our way towards the sea and there, in a wadi, was a camp, not for once of Arabs but of a bunch of bright young Jewish boys and girls, out on a holiday journey like the schoolchildren I had seen in Jericho. They were spending their last day, they told us, of a six-day *tiyul* (hike) all around the wadis nearby. With their portable stoves and tents they were quite self-sufficient in the wilderness or anywhere. They received us with great cries of welcome. We joined them for the evening meal and sat around afterwards singing songs with them. They were starting back for Tel Aviv the next day and were in the greatest spirit—children of every national origin—noisy, brash and warm-hearted.

I saw everything now with paramilitary eyes and thought what useful training this must be for the trouble that might blow up. Somehow the world of politics was closing in again. Josef, I noticed, was sitting quietly in a corner talking to their leader. A group of children gathered round me, asking about life in England, and laughing at my rather archaic Hebrew pronunciation. We accepted their invitation to sleep under canvas with them, and I slept like a log.

★ ★ ★

I suppose that that night was the turning point. Whatever was to happen had been laid down by Providence, so to speak, to start sounding its warning the next day. What did happen was a shot fired in anger. I had heard about odd shooting—something that happened to other people, like everything else. But this time I heard the ping of a bullet on a rock next to my head.

The day had started with the bustle of breaking camp and cheerful talk over coffee. I was sitting near the tent with about six of the boys and girls, holding the hot tin cup gratefully in my hand and loving the husky bantering tone of their young voices. One of the girls—Huldah—was particularly pretty: about fifteen, blonde, tremendously buxom and very shy; and the boys were teasing her about the Arabs they had met during the hike who had always singled her out for their ogling and rude shouts—as unfortunately Arabs (and Italians) have a way of doing.

'How will you like life in the harem?' one of the boys called.

'The young sheikh with the gold kafiyeh—that was the one she liked.'

'When she fell behind and we had to rescue her.'

'Oh Asher!' she pleaded.

'I thought it was the priest,' said one of the boys.

'He certainly fell for her. Did you see his big black beard shaking?'

'I could see his cross jumping up and down.'

'When he stretched out his arms towards her.'

'He was just trying to reassure me,' Huldah said shyly.

'Such reassurance! Did you see that smile?'

'That's how it always starts.'

'The priests. They're the worst. . . .'

The talk of the priest was somehow intriguing. 'A priest out there?' I asked.

'When we were in the Wadi Mukta,' Asher said. 'He was with a merchant, visiting the sheikh.'

'That's where we had such trouble,' another told me. 'There were a few of them on a hill crowded round a cave, and when we got near they started throwing stones.'

'And the priest was so nice to dear little Huldah. . . .' And on they went with their teasing.

It struck me as a little unusual and I went over to Josef and Meir. 'It might be they had arms hidden there,' Josef said.

'Or hashish,' said Meir.

'And the priest?'

'Oh, the merchant was presumably a Christian Arab—probably from Bethlehem. Brought his priest along. Don't ask me why.'

'But suppose they'd found some old manuscripts in a cave and offered to sell them to a merchant. Might he not have brought a priest along to examine them?'

'He might indeed,' Josef said, his eyes narrowing. 'Do you want to go back and look?'

'I wouldn't mind.'

'I wonder how far it was. Have we time?'

'I have time if you have. Let's ask exactly where it was.'

I wondered later if they ever believed in the manuscripts. It was probably enough for them, if they heard of some trouble, to want to examine it. Perhaps they wanted to have another look at old paths. Or perhaps they were just being kind to me. For whatever reason, they got the details and prepared to go back. Within half an hour we had waved good-bye to the children, who had set off for Tel Aviv and the Passover. We had become the children of Israel again, wandering in the wilderness.

'It should take about four hours of fast walking,' Josef had said when he got the details. In fact it took five hours or more before we were in the area, and then another hour before we had identified the spot leading to the place where the crowd of Arabs had gathered, and which was now deserted. It was a long walk, with only two short breaks for rest. But somehow with this clear objective it was no great strain. I was presumably getting into training.

In one sense it was all the same kind of country in which we had been wandering for three days. But it was beginning to look different to me. Whereas before it had been an endless wilderness of rocks and bushes and lizards, it now began to be a series of places with rocks one would recognize later, paths that led somewhere, shapes against the skyline that had their own character, calling out, almost, for some personal name. Even the stillness was no longer absolute. I could listen now for sounds: at night I might have heard voices.

Stooping to pick up an odd-shaped rock, I dislodged some others that led to a rattle of stones down the hill. Josef, leading us in single file, turned his head back to me. 'Better go quietly,' he said. 'Never can tell. If they *have* something hidden here, no point in advertising ourselves.'

Meir behind me had been humming quietly to himself. He now fell silent. I think we had all begun to feel that we might be getting somewhere at last.

The children had told us of a ledge half-way up a precipice, and of a path which led towards it, starting behind a pile of stones that might have been a ruined hut. We had found the stones and were on our way up the path. Ahead, further up, we had just spotted what seemed like the entrance to a cave when the first shot rang out.

I didn't need Josef's quick word to get down. I was flat on the ground instantly, behind a large rock; but I was cold with fright—icy cold. I had heard the bullet strike the rock right near my head, with a puff of rock-dust spinning off and a short succession of sharp sounds as the bullet bounced off and dislodged some other stones. I looked at Josef and Meir, down on the ground beside me. We were lucky to be in a usefully defensive spot. Behind was the sheer rock face, and our sheltering boulder was high enough to hide behind. They were both unbuckling their rucksacks, and I saw them produce heavy ugly-looking revolvers. It was no longer surprising. Nothing would ever be surprising now after that first shot.

We waited for a while and then Josef picked up a stone and threw it on one side to see if there would be any response. It was as natural as in a Western: there was an instant shot towards the place where the stone landed. But we had caught a brief glimpse of a white-clad arm from across the gully raising the rifle. Josef rested his revolver on the ledge before him and took careful aim. He nodded to Meir who threw a second stone. Again the white arm flashed briefly into the sun, and Josef fired. There was a pause, and then another shot came back.

'Sounds like just one of them,' Josef muttered. 'But we can't stay here. They'll hear the shots and come to help. We've got to split up. You go off with Meir,' he said to me, 'and I'll stay on for a bit here and then join you.'

I began to remonstrate, but it was an order. Meir and I began to work our way down the path, almost on hands and knees. Behind us we heard a shot from Josef and an answering shot from the Arab. We had managed to get about four hundred yards away before we heard another shot from Josef, but nothing this time in reply.

'Perhaps he's gone off,' Meir whispered. 'Let's get behind that rock down there and I'll try and draw his fire.'

We slithered on, and in shelter once more Meir took out his revolver and tried a shot towards the area where the Arab had seemed to be. There was no reply. Looking up the path, we saw that Josef had understood and was joining us. We began to descend the path together, hurriedly clinging to shelter when we could. In half an hour we were in the open away from the cave area and feeling safe. Shortly after we came across a couple of young Arab boys with some sheep grazing quietly on a slope, and went over to speak to them. It was all back to normal. They exchanged the usual greetings. 'We're all right now,' Josef said. 'Let's get on.' And on we went by the quickest way we could find on the map to bring us to the Dead Sea littoral.

It had seemed to take an eternity, but it was still only four o'clock when we were down walking by the sea. From then on, safe but exhausted, and very silent, we worked our way north, hoping for a lift at some point. I was keeping going now only by an intense effort of will. My bones seemed to generate an overwhelming ache, and I could hardly keep my eyes open; but I kept up with them. It was eight o'clock, under the full moon, before we found a lift that took us up to Kallia and thence to Jericho. There was a room at the hotel that we could all use. I fell on to the bed, unable to think what it all meant, either in practical terms or to me. I was just longing to sleep, and to get home—to Jerusalem—anywhere.

★ ★ ★

JERUSALEM

There was a pile of letters and messages waiting in my flat: a little package from Heather that had taken three weeks to come by sea—a book of poems with a brief letter; a roughly scrawled message from Shapiro saying that he was driving with Dov to the south on Sunday and would gladly take me along; a formal invitation from the University to the inaugural lecture by the new Professor of History: the subject was certainly rather bizarre in these surroundings: *Some Reflections on Thomas Sprat and the Foundation of the Royal Society*. . . . Ah well. There were two other letters from the University—a request from the librarian for the return of a book, and an invitation to a teaparty. And there was a note from Yael, saying how sorry she had been not to be able to stay on in Jericho, and reminding me not to be late for the Seder.

I looked at the work on my desk, feeling some satisfaction at seeing how much I had done on my book. The translation and introduction were nearly complete, but some of the notes were still full of difficulties. I began to work on one of them, feeling a special kind of relief to plunge into something quite concrete— as dry and dusty as I could make it. It was a discussion of currency questions in the Midrash. As soon as I got into it I began to feel it taking hold of me. I remembered that Robert Graves had said once, when asked about *I Claudius*, that it had something to do with his feeling for coins. Whenever he wrote anything historical, he liked to have coins of the period around him to look at, to touch. Coins were real things: they had passed from hand to hand: they reflected needs, desires, quarrels: the way they were made—the drawings and inscriptions—told one everything of the time. Perhaps he might have added: *and the way they are discovered*; for as I began to struggle with the note, I thought suddenly of Malcah holding the worn little *pruta* in her hand and looking out proudly over the field in which they had found it.

It was easy enough to begin writing about the coins themselves and list some of the exchange values recorded in the Talmud—*4 prutas equal one silver denarius, 25 denarii equal one aureus*, and so on with many other coins. But as soon as one looked into it one became aware of constant changes in values at different times and in different places—of coins going in and out of circulation for commercial reasons, for political reasons, and even for moral reasons, such as when the Jews after the Bar Cochba Revolt tried to hide all the coins of the time of Trajan and Hadrian because they might have been made of gold looted by the Romans from the Temple, so that to use them would be sacrilege. On the other side were the attempts of the Romans to get rid of some Bar Cochba coins because he had defaced the Emperor's portrait on them. And what was I to make of the dictum in the Talmud of the leading rabbi of the second century, who first taught: '*Silver coins acquire gold*', but later, in his old age, reversed his teaching to read: '*Gold coins acquire silver*'. Did this imply some heavy movements of bullion across the Mediterranean during this period leading to a change-around in the relative value of gold and silver? I knew that Heichelheim had published some interesting material on this subject, and I would have to pursue it for my note. It suddenly occurred to me how much more real this all was—how much more within my compass—than the fantasy pursuit of Biblical manuscripts in desert caves. . . .

The day had practically gone by the time I pushed my books away and got ready for the party. I might have spent the afternoon wandering in the Old City to see the Easter processions, but these hours of study had been better for me. I had needed to shut my mind off Yael until I saw her. It might be a different Yael now—or a different me: I could understand that. But when she came over in the entrance hall of her house to take my hand, and hold it for a moment, softly, I knew that I was as close to her—and always would be—as on that first morning when she stood at my door.

The two adjoining rooms of the ground floor were filled with a special table stretching their entire length and sparkling with silver and candlelight. The mood inside that warm, gay house seemed to have shut out all that was baleful and hag-ridden in the world outside. It was a Jewish Feast of Freedom that we had come to celebrate—a mixed assortment of Jews, ingathered from

JERUSALEM

all nations, a batch of Christians—Government officials and scholars—and, as expected, three selected Arabs, bolstered, with great appropriateness, by a visitor from Egypt—a cotton merchant who did a large business, I was told, with Jewish textile manufacturers in Palestine.

Hardcastle was there among the officials—his first Seder, he told me. I gave him a short explanation of the proceedings to follow. Among the Jewish visitors was one of my favourite professors from the University, a lightly bearded Frenchman, whose lectures on Roman Syria I had been attending occasionally. I moved across to ask him about coins, and he plunged into a long disquisition on the rivalries between the mints of Antioch and Tyre. He sat down next to me for the long service that preceded the meal, and enlivened the recital—as Jewish tradition prescribes one should—with a constant stream of footnotes and queries on the familiar story it unfolds of the villainy of Pharaoh and the triumph of Moses.

In my childhood the service had been endless: it had seemed to me that we would never get to the food. But here, with Christians and Arabs following everything with rapt attention, it seemed to make things more engrossing for the Jews too, and we were soon through the rituals and on to the dinner itself. Yael, at the foot of the table, seemed almost transcendentally happy; but I noticed that as the real wine began to be served—as distinct from the sacramental *four cups*—she was drinking very freely, and talking at a higher pitch than was usual for her. If Sirov, at the other end, noticed, he gave no sign, bending forward courteously to his neighbours, and drawing in others around him to the conversation—the perfect host, but so much more: a man who was at such peace with himself that he blessed the troubled air around him. It was as if he touched each one of us at a point where there was love to respond with instead of frustration.

I felt it most clearly at the end of the evening when, with almost all the guests gone, I stood with him—and with Yael and Hardcastle—at the open french window, looking out over the moonlit garden. I had been ready to leave with the others, but

Yael had motioned to me to stay, with Hardcastle. It was a little puzzling, but I was soon told the reason. 'The Inspector has offered to take us all on his midnight round,' she said gaily. She was still sparkling with a kind of feverish liveliness. 'He walks round the Old City at midnight. Won't you come?'

'Oh, I'd love to,' I said.

'You'll come too, Alex,' she said.

'Ah no, Yael. If I might be excused. I will stay here looking at the garden. I still have one last Seder duty, you know.'

'The Song of Songs?'

'Of course.'

She laughed, put her arms around his neck from behind, and gave him a fond hug. 'Well, I'll run upstairs and change. I can't walk in this.' She was wearing a handsome evening frock of deep red. 'I won't be a minute.'

Sirov had taken up an old leather-bound Bible and was showing it to Hardcastle while Yael went off. 'It's part of the tradition,' he said. 'The rabbis were never really happy about having the Song of Songs included in the Bible. Too romantic. But they allowed one to read it on Seder night. After all—a song of love and spring. It's a good night for it, wouldn't you say?'

We stood silently, looking out at the shimmering light and breathing the scented air.

'We're not really fair to the rabbis,' he said. 'We think of them as dry and legalistic—and this is what they were in their writing. But it's not bad for a man to have something clear-cut and practical to be absorbed in—something that really stretches the mind. A man can get a little rocky if he's not anchored down in something—whether it's science, or business, or the law. I don't think it stopped the rabbis being human.'

We were still silent. Hardcastle lit a cigarette, and we stood there. Sirov went on musing quietly.

'The Song of Songs,' he said. 'Romantic love. The rabbis couldn't bear romantic love—not for long stretches anyhow. Yet they were absorbed by love: they had a clear idea of what it meant—its dangers as well as its joys. Come to think of it, they showed their real attitude to love in one very simple way—they rarely talked about it. Love isn't a thing you talk about. Not a bad start, was it? When they do talk about it, they express one other idea: love has to be unpossessive if it is to be real. There's a saying in the *Ethics of the Fathers*'—he turned to me—'you must have recited it many times, I expect. . . .'

'Undoubtedly,' I agreed, 'without understanding a word of it.'

'No, I expect you didn't. I didn't either, but it grows on one. How should one translate it? It says'—he turned to Hardcastle— 'the love that is dependent is not real love: only the love that leaves a person independent lasts for ever. It's not easy to translate, but I think that's what they meant.'

It had come back to me. 'Do you remember the two examples they gave—from the Bible?' I asked.

'Yes, the examples are interesting. The first is Amnon and Tamar, obsessive love. This isn't love at all, but a sickness. Amnon is obsessed by his sister—really his half-sister—Tamar. Of course the way it's told in Samuel is quite masterly, isn't it? He is utterly obsessed by her. He can't eat. He's pale with longing. He dreams night and day of possessing her. Finally he forces her to yield to him: and then he hates her.'

'And the other example?' Hardcastle asked.

Sirov smiled gently. 'Just as interesting. The love of David and Jonathan. I don't know how the rabbis envisaged it. The Bible says that as young men their love for each other surpassed that of a man for a woman. But to the rabbis it was quite innocent—an unforced, unshakeable kind of love: and David's lament on Jonathan's death comes through that way. They had gone their separate ways—led their own lives. But whether they were together or separate, their love for each other had never wavered. And it was a love that survived death. . . .'

We heard Yael coming downstairs, and Sirov looked at her affectionately. She had put on a skirt and a short loose coat, and had changed her shoes.

'Have a good walk,' he said, waving to us. 'I will sit here and read my Song of Songs.'

MEMOIRS OF A SPECIAL CASE

Outside we got into Hardcastle's big black Lancia and drove down to the Old City.

★ ★ ★

We were up on the top of the wall when it happened. We had spent almost an hour wandering through the alleys and squares of the Old City itself, apparently deserted but, under Hardcastle's guidance, bursting with life. He had taken us first into the Church of the Holy Sepulchre, pushing his way with authority through the throngs gathered in the glittering clustered chapels, the air full of incense and tinkling bells and strange passionate murmurings in many tongues. To a stranger pushing through it was a bewildering sight, with priests of all the competing sects fighting for their turn, each surrounded by his faithful—pilgrims from far and near, the men in fine clothes, the women kerchiefed—dizzy with the excitement of the long-awaited moment. Wherever we went, the police on duty saluted Hardcastle smartly. He would exchange a quick word and move on. In the other parts of the City where we went after the Church, he strode quickly down the streets, pushing open a door abruptly here and there, taking a quick look and walking on. It seemed as if there were many things going on that he tolerated but kept under his watch. At one point he pushed open a door and motioned us into a large steamy room which proved to be a kind of Turkish bath, with men squealing happily to see a woman, however briefly. Then with the tour of duty over, we had climbed to the top of the wall and walked round a little. The moonlight was almost piercingly bright after the dark alleys below. The valleys, with their old stones and cypresses, glistened with an unearthly glow. Down below, on the south side, was a Bedouin camp. We looked down at the brown tents nestling in the shadow of the wall and with only the occasional bray of a camel breaking the silence. It had a pearly clarity and beauty.

I stood there, resting my arms on the parapet, unable to tear myself away for a moment, while Hardcastle and Yael moved on. It seemed as if one could stay there in the fresh night air for ever. There were no thoughts in my mind, but merely a feeling of elevation—a timeless feeling, as when one looks out at night over a calm sea. I may have stood there for ten minutes or more, alone.

Finally I shook myself free and turned to follow. They had disappeared round a bend in the wall, and it was when I came to the corner where a battlement jutted out that I saw them, transfixed by their own feeling, and oblivious to everything else. They were standing facing each other, holding each other's hands. She was looking up at him in a way that said everything: he held her hands and looked down at her, both standing quite still. I turned back quickly with a sick, hollow feeling and stood where I had waited before, looking down at the Bedouin.

So much was clear now—so many things buried or half buried: the meeting at Ain Harif—she had to be where he was; Jericho, the sudden change of plan after the phone call. . . . I wondered if it had started through her link with the underground: she had been told to keep an eye on Hardcastle the policeman. Had it started that way? Yes, it probably had, but what did it matter now? I had seen the way she looked at him.

I gripped the stone parapet hard enough to hurt my hand. There was a raging jealousy in me. It was wrong—wrong. I remembered her wild feverish eyes at the Seder. She was possessed. I turned round, trembling, to go to her—to save her—and at that moment I heard their footsteps. They were coming back, and had turned the corner of the wall.

'Isn't it marvellous?' Yael called.

'Marvellous,' I called back.

Hardcastle was smiling quietly as he always did. 'Shall we go?' he asked.

'Oh yes,' I said. 'Let's go.'

We climbed down the steps and walked round to his car. On the way there we had sat all three in the front, but now I got into the back seat. As the car took off, Yael turned towards me and I looked at her. She looked back at me and could see that I knew. Her face took on a terrible sadness as she looked up at me mutely. Her hand was resting on the back of the seat and I put my hand over hers and pressed it softly. We sat that way while the car roared through the silent streets up to her house. And then, turning the corner into her road, we saw police cars, lights, and a crowd standing outside. Hardcastle's look had gone grim as he swung the car to the door and leapt out. The British policeman standing there recognized him and saluted.

'It's Mr Sirov, sir. He's dead. Shot.'

'How?'

'An Arab. Half an hour ago. The patrol you ordered was on its round just after the shot and they caught him. Mr Sirov had been sitting at the open window with the light on, reading. Absolute sitting duck. Shot through the heart. It's political. The Arab's a member of that extremist party. They hated Sirov.'

Yael had run into the house. I ran in after her, and when she saw me she turned to me and buried her head on my shoulder, clinging to me and sobbing wildly.

★ ★ ★

The hours passed while she sobbed and clung to me, until finally the doctor put her to sleep with a sedative. But on the next day when I saw her she had already changed. The life had drained from her face. She was calm and brief with me. It was the same until after the funeral. And then, taking my hand and holding it for a minute, she said simply: 'Good-bye.'

On the day of the funeral there was another assassination—in Haifa; and from then on it was a mounting story of shooting and destruction. The Arab Revolt had started. I read about it in the papers after I left. When I was back in England, I had a letter from my friend the French professor sending me an article he had promised me. He wrote sadly of the Seder we had shared —'the last night of freedom'—and went on to talk of Yael. She had given up the house, he said, and gone away from Jerusalem. I learnt later that she had gone to work full-time as a commander with the Haganah.

Shapiro had been sad to see me go. I had greeted him morosely when he came to see me, but it was impossible to be morose for long in his company. These things happened, he said. There would be worse to come: much worse. But why be depressed about it? Life went on. The whole point of life was that you suffered and made the best of it. It was the positive things that mattered. Take my book, for example. I had written something, so something had come out of all this. What about the manuscripts? Had I found anything on my trip to the Dead Sea?

I told him about my wanderings among the caves, and in particular, of course, about the caves where we had seemed to be on the track of something. We looked carefully at a map together so that he could guide cousin Hermann to the possibilities there. 'What do you think the Arabs were hiding there?' I asked him. 'Could it really be hashish?'

'What do you know about hashish?' he asked me suspiciously.

'Me? I don't know anything. It was Meir, one of the men with me, who mentioned it. I know that that's the area for smuggling things from Transjordan.'

'Does it have to be hashish?'

'Well, there must be a lot of profit in hasish. A small packet could probably make one a fortune.'

'There's a lot that goes on down there,' he said. 'It's better sometimes not to ask.'

'Arms, too?'

'Arms? Yes. And other things they bring in. You'd be surprised. It's like in Bible times. They bring things from Damascus —from Baghdad—even up from the Red Sea. . . .'

'And cousin Hermann isn't just bottling Dead Sea water. . . .'

'Well,' he said reluctantly, 'it's a good spot to watch things happening. We could put him on the track with those caves.'

'Wouldn't it be a bit hard now, with all this shooting?'

'Yes, it would. But it will blow over. The British Government may be stupid, but they're not stupid enough to let the Arabs tear the country apart.'

'But what's the solution?'

'Solution? Is there ever a solution? I know only one thing. Life must go on. And you'll come back. I know. And this time when you come back, you will not be so innocent, eh? More practical. There's so much we could do together. . . .'

The letter with the poems from Heather was a month old. She had talked about the usual things—entertainments to keep her busy—books—the spring. But now, when I was getting ready to leave, there was suddenly a telegram from her which brought me rapidly up-to-date: 'TERRIBLY HAPPY ENGAGED GEORGE MARRYING WHITSUN GEORGE VICAR SEATON ABBAS WONDERFUL NORMAN CHURCH QUEEN ANNE VICARAGE MUST COME NEED YOUR BLESSING LOVE.' I sent her my blessing, and six weeks later I went down from Oxford to Dorset to see her married, radiantly happy.

It is all so long ago, and I thought it was time I wrote something that would remind me of those days. So many of the people are dead now. Malcah was shot as a terrorist by the British in 1947. Yael was killed in 1948 during the War of Independence. Not everything died. Israel is alive. As Josef said: 'Not all prophecies come true, but some do.' Perhaps one should mention something else that died: Sirov's hope for understanding. I suppose that died with him on Seder night.

And Shapiro? I thought of him, of course, when the first stories of the discovery of the Dead Sea Scrolls began to come out in 1948. My book on the Midrash—with a splendid footnote on currency—had been finished in 1939, accepted for publication by the Oxford Press, and then held up by the war. I would have to reconsider the whole historical framework now if I ever wanted to publish, but the truth was that I had lost heart for Midrash. All my work seemed stale when one thought of the limitless interest of these fantastic Biblical manuscripts. And to have found them in the Wadi Qumran, so close to Kallia! Had Shapiro been involved? Or perhaps cousin Hermann? The story how they had been discovered—and even more how they had been hawked around between merchants and scholars, Bedouin Arabs and Syrian monks—was all so confusing and suspicious. The official story was that a young Arab shepherd boy had come across the first jar in a cave early in 1947 while he was chasing a lost sheep—or taking refuge from a thunderstorm.

JERUSALEM

But there were other legends growing up, and one that I read of spoke of smugglers looking for a new cave to hide things in and coming across the jar. The literature on the Scrolls grew and grew. One day I might be able to work it all into my book. In the meantime I read everything on the subject avidly and finally I had my reward.

It was in a book by Professor Millar Burrows, the first authoritative study, published in 1956. He describes in his first chapter the struggle of two Christian Arab merchants, Khalil Eskander and George Isaiah, to get the Archbishop at the Syrian Orthodox Monastery in Jerusalem to buy the manuscripts. The Archbishop—Athanasius Samuel—was excited and offered to buy. But when George Isaiah finally brought the three Bedouins up from Bethlehem to Jerusalem clutching their precious burden, they were turned away at the door of the monastery by a priest 'who thought that their dirty dilapidated manuscripts were of no interest'. Eskander got in touch again with the Archbishop; and this is how Burrows tells the story:

'*Khalil Eskander told Archbishop Samuel further that when George Isaiah and the Bedouins were sent away from the monastery they proceeded to the square just inside the Jaffa Gate. Here they encountered a Jewish merchant who offered to buy the Scrolls for a good price and asked the Bedouins to come to his office for the money. George Isaiah, however, persuaded them to refuse this offer.*'

And now for my fantasy. Who could this Jewish merchant have been except Shapiro? And if so, how idiotic of him not to have been carrying enough money to do the deal on the spot. Imagine the suspicion of the Bedouins at being asked to accompany a Jewish merchant to his office. Cousin Hermann would never have been caught napping like that. We can be sure that he would have been carrying enough ready cash on him for any surprise deal. Of course I have never tried to verify anything of this. I would be sad to see my fantasies go up in a puff of smoke: so much nicer to cherish them as dreams, like all my memories of Jerusalem.

III

THE SPECIAL CASE

ONE of the joys of being back in England is going down to spend an occasional week-end with Elaine and Neville Blond at their house near Fairbridge. There is a touch of nostalgia in it for me in any case because it brings back the happy—almost carefree—years in New York shortly after the war when I worked with Neville there on developing British exports. But there is more in it than that. Fairbridge for me is still the racecourse.

I have to pass the racecourse directly on the way down. As the short village street slips by and I see the tall familiar gates approaching, I get myself ready for the swift look that I will turn on the long rows of dark green stables before accelerating for the open road that lies ahead and the last three miles before I arrive. I still cannot quite accept the fact that these stables house horses now and not human beings. If someone is in the car with me I begin to wonder as we approach it if I should try to explain. I know I cannot, and resolve to be silent.

For this is my war story, my blitz story—and many other things. I am the sole survivor of what happened there—the Ancient Mariner himself. Perhaps it is odd for me to assume this role, since I was something of an outsider when hundreds of German refugees were imprisoned in this racecourse in 1940. Yet even at the time I knew that, in one sense, this was my experience rather than theirs and that when it was all over the memory of it would be left in my care.

Not that it was in any way grim for me. On the contrary, it was a brilliantly exciting time. Above us they were fighting the Battle of Britain. The sirens would wail from a long way off, with a timing quite unrelated to the planes or vapour trails that we would see winding through the clear blue sky. A few bombs now and then would plough up the harmless fields, and here and there would be the wreckage of a plane, a Heinkel or a Spitfire. Down below, the racecourse hummed with an existence of its own, like some Greek city-state, with its slaves and rulers, endless intrigue, high philosophy and low comedy. Within the encompassing walls, the citizens plotted relentless war against the enemy outside—not the Nazis, of course, but that other, more personal enemy, officialdom.

When I had first met them, they were an anonymous mob to me. Then they had ceased to be a mob and became cases, each of them, in his view, a special case deserving priority. And finally they had stopped being cases and became Kettner the socialist, Stoessel the mechanic, Weissbrot the Talmudist, Kindler the crook, Sommetski the *shlemiel*, and so on in their hundreds. Behind them in London, and pulling all the strings, was Sir Gordon Tyrell, head of the Lord Lieutenant's Office, as unpredictable a guardian of security as England produced even in those unpredictable days.

The German refugees in Britain had been rounded up and interned when France fell, not because they were likely to be sympathetic to Hitler when he landed at Dover but because they seemed an irritatingly alien element in the cosy and familiar society that was cheerfully girding itself to meet invasion. To the refugees, this internment was almost a heavier affront than the anti-Jewish laws which had driven them from Germany. They were insulted and terrified. Dumped suddenly into racecourses in various parts of England, they felt swindled out of the honour due to them as the enemy's first victims, and they were terrified because Hitler was on the doorstep. Some wanted to get out of England as fast as they could, others wanted to be free to fight him, and all of them felt a sense of terror at being cooped up behind high walls, under the supervision of men alien to them —with guns.

Their sense of confusion and fear made them at first sight a pitiable group, or worse, to the major commanding the camp and his officers. Until the refugees arrived, with hardly a day's warning, in a huge convoy of army lorries, Fairbridge Racecourse had been a prison camp for a much more agreeable type of person, the German Nazis whom the authorities had rounded up or captured in the early fights at sea. A fine body of men,

THE SPECIAL CASE

Major Blackwood told me: proud, independent, capable, healthy; a pleasure to look after them. And suddenly he had lost his beloved Nazis and been given these unfit, middle-aged wrecks, whining at their fate, pressing to get out. Above all, there was this constant screaming about their papers, their passports, their visas. They were driving him mad.

He told me this when I arrived, and I could sympathize with his feeling of helplessness. I had been dropped into the situation with equal lack of warning. Sir Gordon Tyrell had sent for me at Oxford, where I had thought to spend a last quiet week before reporting to the R.A.F. My name had come to him somehow; wires had been pulled; the R.A.F. had agreed to wait; and I found myself on my way to Fairbridge. There was a special job to be done there, Tyrell explained. Of the thousands of refugees whom they had locked up in different parts of England and the Isle of Man, a few hundred had been pulled out and sent down to Fairbridge because they claimed to be transmigrants who had visas pending for the United States. Fairbridge, thirty miles south of London, was convenient for access to the U.S. Consulate. My instructions were simple: get their visas for them and get them out of England. The fewer Germans around during an invasion, the better for everybody.

There were, of course, difficulties. For one thing, there was the unfortunate mistake about the passports. When the refugees had been swooped on, one of the instructions given to the police had somehow led to all their most precious documents being taken from them, 'for examination'. These documents, the lifeblood of the harried refugee, had been collected at a central point —some garage in the north of England—and then lost. It was unfortunate. There were also problems of wives, children, and relatives who would have to go too and were not conveniently locked up in a racecourse for easy processing. There was a slight problem of shipping. And finally—something they tended to overlook—there was a war on.

It was this last point that I found myself wanting to express when I entered the racecourse on my first morning, to be swallowed up in a second by the surging crowd of refugees

MEMOIRS OF A SPECIAL CASE

clamouring for their cases to be heard. They had been told that someone was being sent from London to solve their problems, and they wanted to lose no time in telling me what to do. Their visas. Their wives. Their luggage. Why had England done this? They were ill. Their businesses would collapse. They had a brother in desperate danger in France, an uncle in Mexico who should be cabled to. . . .

I tried to bear with it for a while, getting ready for what I knew would be the worst moment of the first day. To help them, I had prepared cards on which they were to give me all the information they could about their families, passports, guarantors, luggage, and so on. New photographs would have to be taken; and then, by collating all this with anything that would come in from other places, such as the refugee organization at Holborn House or the U.S. Consulate, some new documentary personalities could emerge, ready for the sacerdotal stamp of authority. My cards were an essential first step, but when I produced them and explained, shouting out the instructions in my best German from the steps of the Members' Bar, the expected howl of rage arose from the crowd: 'More papers!' 'Enough of papers!' 'They have destroyed our papers!' Behind them, the Tommies watched it all, silent and uncomprehending. The howls began to subside as the cards were passed around and the men disappeared to fill them in. Quiet descended.

Back across the road in Major Blackwood's room an hour later, I took a grateful swig at the tall whisky and soda that he put before me. We were sitting drinking silently when I happened to put my hand into my pocket and found that something like a dozen notes had apparently been palmed on me, presumably during the first rush of the crowd. They were almost all of a pattern: 'Please help me.' 'I am a special case.' 'My wife is ill: unless I am freed . . .' Full names, date and place of birth and other biographical details were meticulously appended. But one was a carefully written note in German and unsigned. It said:

'We were almost all rescued from Nazi concentration camps through the help of England. This we will not forget. Now I have read

THE SPECIAL CASE

in the Manchester Guardian *three days ago that a debate was held in Parliament on the internment. The Government said that a mistake had been made and would be put right as soon as possible. In the middle of a war, the English Parliament takes time to defend the homeless refugee. This we will not forget.*'

I showed the note to the major and translated it for him.

'Hm,' he grunted. 'No signature, eh? Doesn't want any favours. Now that's what I call a really special case.'

★   ★   ★

It was two weeks before I was ready for the first bus-load to go up to the U.S. Consulate in London to see about visas, and then it was only by working very long hours in the stable we had set aside as an office. During this time, documents had been pouring in from relatives, refugee organizations, and consulates all over the world. Fifteen of the refugees had been organized into a clerical staff under a man I had selected for the job—Baumgart, a quiet former insurance official, who ran the office stable with Teutonic efficiency. To maintain contact, I was dashing up and down between Fairbridge and London on a motor-bike I had nobbled from the Army, with saddlebags chock-full of cards and papers. In London, with the blitz taking hold, it was becoming impossible to get around easily except on something like a motor-bike, and I had many people to see, in many government departments, to get the whole thing moving. My London visits over and my saddlebags filled again, I would start back for Fairbridge with a sense of expectant happiness, opening up the bike on the deserted roads to glorious bursts of speed, and then slowing down through the village and purring up to the racecourse gates as if I were coming home. Hearing the engine, the refugees would gather inside the gate and surround me as I got off stiffly, some of them still pushing forward with unbearable anxiety, others pushing for the sake of it, and a small number smiling unconcernedly or calling out laughingly, 'Can I drive to London?' or 'I'm a special case.'

One of the refugees, an Austrian engineer called Stoessel, had made himself the mechanic in charge of the bike, and he took it over from me as I got off, to give it a little loving care, as a groom takes away a horse. If ever a man had been victimized by an administrative bungle, it was Stoessel—plump, gentle, and uncomplaining. He was an engineer of a high order and had been working on Rolls-Royce aeroplane engines when war broke out. Because of his skill and certain inventions that he had sent to the Admiralty, a special stamp had been put into his passport stating *Essential to the War Effort*, a tribute that was his undoing. The police, swooping down on him in a Derbyshire village on that fatal day, had been so determined to take care of clever Germans who might be agents in disguise that they had arrested not only him but also his wife, sending her down for safe-keeping to Wandsworth Gaol. And now his papers were lost and he had become the guardian of my motor-bike.

Baumgart, prissy but competent, would unload the papers from my saddlebags, and a crowd would follow us to the stable. Inevitably, when I got there, I would find that half a dozen notes had been stuffed into my pockets. I got used to it. We would settle down to work: our first solid list of emigrants was taking shape; a ship on which I had been allotted sixty places would be sailing in a week. The wrangling for places was already in full spate.

There were other problems too. The government, fulfilling its promise to Parliament, had announced certain categories of immediate release. Some of the refugees were leaving Fairbridge, others were arriving, and the other racecourses were being combed for emigrants. The commandant complained that this state of uncertainty interfered with camp discipline. The refugees complained that the food was uneatable. Added to these were the fights within the camp itself. In one stable there was a huge map of the Lowlands and France, and bitter arguments took place there on Nazi strategy and Allied tactics. Under the grandstand, the Orthodox Jews among the refugees had set up a synagogue; opposite, as if to annoy them, a group of Marxists led by Kettner, the famous German socialist, had got hold of a typewriter and was putting out a camp newspaper.

THE SPECIAL CASE

The routine of prison life had, in other words, taken hold, though I hardly understood at first into what a marvellous historical pattern these things arrange themselves. But I was soon to learn. With the first bus-load almost prepared, I was sitting one day in my stable working on the papers with great intensity, oblivious of the fact that the lunch hour had come and gone, when a young boy, neatly dressed in a white coat, arrived at my door bearing a note in a stiff white envelope. The notepaper, equally impressive, carried a simple message: 'Mr Rado Kindler and his associates will be happy if you will take lunch with them today.' It was clearly not an invitation but a command.

I accompanied the young man across the compound to a room in the bowels of the grandstand, where I found a dark, slim, and very well-dressed man of about thirty-five waiting to receive me, with the exact air of a *maître d'hôtel*. This, in fact, was what he was. The task he had been given in the camp, presumably by choice, was to organize the feeding arrangements. When the public bout was over, he and a select few retired to this quiet little room behind the kitchen, where lunch was served to them, in a style appropriate to their station, by some of his menials. It was perhaps a simple lunch that they put before me: some *paté*, a steak, strawberries and cream. The *vin* was *ordinaire*, but the brandy and cigars were rather fine. Then the others discreetly retired, and I was left alone with the radiant Mr Kindler.

He brushed aside my questions with an elegant wave of the hand. 'One has to organize oneself,' he said carelessly. 'But I wonder if I might ask for your advice. You see, I have three ways of securing my release and am not sure which will be the swiftest or the best for me. I could claim release on medical grounds immediately. I have several doctors' certificates. But I am also pursuing release for emigration, and if I get released on medical grounds first, this might affect my American visa, don't you think? The other way is to claim release under the category of running a business essential for the war effort. I could arrange this quite easily, since I have a factory which makes protective head covering.'

'Protective head covering?' I asked. 'Steel helmets?'

He smiled. 'I will have to see what contracts I get.'

'But your factory?'

'I have thirty girls making hats in Bond Street. I would switch them over and expand. That is no problem. No, the only problem is which form of release to claim. You may say, claim all. But the medical claim is a bit tricky for the American visa, and if I am released to run the factory, will the British authorities hold back my exit visa? It is not an easy problem, you will agree?'

'It's one you will have to solve yourself,' I said. 'I haven't seen your name so far on the visa list.'

'Oh, Baumgart will see to that,' he said confidently. 'Please don't trouble yourself with the details. You work too hard. Work of this kind should be left to others. Some of us have more important things to do. You must go? So happy to have had the pleasure of your company. I hope you will allow me to offer you lunch again soon.'

Kindler had a good effect on me. Instead of rushing back to my stable, I slowed down a bit and wandered around the passages under the grandstand. I thought that I might have a chat, perhaps, with Kettner, but there was no one there when I looked into the camp newspaper room. From the room opposite, though, I heard voices, and I pushed open the door. There were six or seven men inside, all wearing caps, sitting in a half-circle around a heavily bearded figure, Rabbi Weissbrot, a famous scholar whom I had already met over the problem of his visa. They looked up as I came in but seemed to have no objection to my presence, and I sat down at the back to listen. The room, which was furnished in shiny mahogany, with photographs of racehorses everywhere, looked out directly on the course, glowing in the afternoon sun.

I heard the rabbi's first words as he resumed and for a brief second felt a chill of the supernatural in my spine. Of all books, he was reading the Midrash on Lamentations. But in the same moment I realized why. It was July. The Fast of Ab would be just about due—the anniversary of the destruction of the Temple.

THE SPECIAL CASE

On the Ninth of Ab the Orthodox Jews in the camp would read the Book of Lamentations, sitting on low stools, with the ashes of mourning in their hair; and by custom in the weeks before they read the Midrash and other similar books to prepare for the solemnity of the Fast. How remote it all seemed to me now, and how close. If it had not been for the war my own study of this Midrash would have been out by now. I had been furious at the delay, but perhaps the Oxford Press had after all done me a kindness in sending the manuscript back to me on the day war had broken out. They had explained that all books of scholarship not connected directly with the war effort would now have to be suspended. But no manuscript back in the author's hands can ever stay suspended. It becomes clay again to be worked on. And here in the grandstand at Fairbridge I could see what was wrong. Rabbi Weissbrot's commentary on the Midrash was quite different from my own.

I was not ashamed of my work. I had put a lot into it—a lot of thought and knowledge and research. I had examined word forms and parallels: I had established a critical text: I had pursued in my notes all kinds of literary and historical allusions. I had given it everything possible, in fact, except one thing—faith. And for Rabbi Weissbrot, sitting with his friends under the grandstand at Fairbridge Racecourse, and calmly discussing what the work meant, this was the only thing that mattered.

When the Second Temple was destroyed by the Romans in A.D. 70, the Rabbi Weissbrot of that time gathered a few of his friends around him, quietly, at Yavneh, and sat down amid the ruins of all they had loved to try and understand God's purpose. There was only one way that they knew, but it was infallible. If one accepted that the Bible spoke for all human history and not merely for the particular moment in time when it was written, one had simply to keep on studying the Bible and all would be clear. If one failed to achieve peace of mind one was simply not studying deeply enough. One wasn't listening.

The whole thing was timeless. Lamentations described the Destruction of the First Temple, by Nebuchadnezzar. It was just as appropriate to the Second Destruction by Titus; and now everything they read, in the book itself or the Midrash on it, applied with equal force to the world of Hitler. With no sense of anger or complaint, they were seeking to understand God's purpose in all that had happened to them—and not merely to them, but to their ancestors. If they could understand God's purpose, they could identify themselves with it. Human history was an endless story with only one clear clue to hold on to and pursue, the role of the Jews. The Jews had a special role in God's Providence. They were, in fact, a special case.

I wandered back to my stable. There was a telephone message from the head of the refugee organization at Holborn House. They had heard from Sir Gordon Tyrell's office that the first bus would be sent down the next day to take the fifty most likely visa candidates to London. We were on our way.

★ ★ ★

The next three weeks were a fantastic medley of coming and going. In general, everyone was being helpful. The Americans were leaning over backwards in the granting of visas wherever their rules on guarantors could somehow be met. Tyrell was waving aside every regulation of Whitehall whenever I turned to him to cut some red tape. Behind us, Holborn House was a massive bulwark in absorbing the pressure from wives, children, friends, and relatives. Even Goering was helping us by keeping air raids to a reasonable level, or at least by staging them according to a timetable that didn't get in our way too much.

The first group of refugees was herded on to a train at Euston one dark night and disappeared north into the blackout, towards their boat at Liverpool, with an air of triumph that made it seem like the Exodus from Egypt. One wondered vaguely what they would make of their Promised Land. If the Bible was any guide, there would be a good deal of murmuring in the wilderness, and the Promised Land itself might not be quite so golden as they thought. Perhaps one day they would look back, not exactly to the fleshpots of England, but at least to some of its

THE SPECIAL CASE

virtues. But, for the moment, life had only one purpose for them—to get out. They had had enough of Europe. America was a land of peace and plenty. They would start a new life, until Nebuchadnezzar or Titus appeared again.

There was no time to organize this exodus with any ease or exactness. It was not only the children of Israel who were after me to get things moving. Pharaoh himself, in the form of Sir Gordon Tyrell, had sent for me one day to tell me that whatever could be done should be done quickly, as transport was getting increasingly scarce. The Nazi submarines were taking their toll, lying in wait on the eastern run across the Atlantic for the ships heavily laden with food and war supplies from America. The whole refugee operation might have to end very soon.

Without being told, those who were at Fairbridge seemed to know this, and the intrigues to get on the lists—first for the daily run to London to go to the Consulate, and then, more difficult by far, to get a berth on a ship—grew more intense. Try as we did to convey the feeling that there was no favouritism and that everything done in the stables was handled strictly according to the studbook, there was a constant murmuring, and every day I found personal letters of complaint for me or notes stuffed into my pocket. Baumgart was a tower of strength through all this struggle. He deliberately kept himself off the lists, and his calm Teutonic efficiency was probably more convincing than my fairly obvious flexibility and sentimentality. But even Baumgart had his soft spot. He asked me privately one day if we could do something for one of the helpers in the office, a man called Sommetski, whose father was already in America and very ill with cancer. I had seen Sommetski around. He was a dumb-looking creature, generating a feeling of mute helplessness. From what Baumgart told me, I realized that he was one of those people for whom things always went wrong. He had had an American visa sent to him in Germany, but it had arrived after he left and expired before he could use it. Another visa was on its way when his guarantor suddenly died. He had arranged everything and secured a passage from England just before the war, when his small child had caught measles. Baumgart was trying hard to help him, but somehow it was impossible to push him forward.

My own favourite was Stoessel. His wife was still in Wandsworth Gaol. The authorities had not yet produced the information on his special work that would release him, and he was therefore relying on his emigration release. In the meantime, he went about his work smilingly and without complaint, polishing my motor-bike until every part gleamed like silver, and never asking for any kind of special attention. I was quite delighted one day when, looking through the lists, I saw that his visa was finally due to be granted and that his priority had given him and his wife berths on the next ship. When I told him about the berths, he glowed with relief.

I went across to see Baumgart and found him talking to Sommetski, who was sitting on a chair with a look of abject misery on his face. Baumgart took me aside to tell me that a cable had just come in from the refugee organization in New York advising that Sommetski's father was desperately ill and could not last long. Sommetski's priority would not entitle him to go on the next ship, and we had no idea when there would be another one. Was there anyone we could ask to surrender his place?

I thought I knew who would and went to find Stoessel. I explained that if he gave up his berths in favour of the Sommetskis, there was no guarantee that we could get him off later. He smiled in his soft Austrian way. 'Of course I'll stand down,' he said. 'If you can get my wife out of gaol without the emigration, that will be enough. We will wait. I will go back to work if they will give me the permit. Let Sommetski go.' Later in the day I saw Sommetski talking to Stoessel, or rather just looking at him in dumb gratitude.

★ ★ ★

I thought that all was now well. I should have known better. Fate does not let go of its hapless ones so easily.

THE SPECIAL CASE

At first it was just the feeling that our luck was turning. For one thing, Goering had become unreasonable again, and it was becoming extremely awkward to get around London because of the constant alerts and the holes in the roads that forced traffic into elaborate detours. Assembling the party at Holborn House for what might be our last shipment proved unusually difficult. There was an increasing fractiousness in the air.

The train was to leave Euston for Glasgow at 5.30 that evening, with the ship due to sail in the early hours of the next morning. There had been a constant procession of the emigrants all day through Holborn House. At 4.0 I was sitting in the room of one of the directors, drinking a cup of tea and edging carefully into a final sense of relief, when the news I had half been waiting for reached us. An agitated secretary burst in.

'Sommetski!' she wailed. 'He and his wife! They're outside with their child. They've lost their papers. Left them on the bus.'

We rushed out into the main hall. Mrs Sommetski had fainted and was lying on the floor, where they were trying to revive her. The child was whimpering. Sommetski stood there, wringing his hands in a terrible unending movement of despair.

'I had all the papers in a little bag,' he said. 'Our passports, visas, ship tickets, everything. We were in the bus coming here from the Marble Arch. I was holding the bag very tight not to lose it. And when we got here, I didn't have it. I must have left it in the bus. And now all is lost.' He twisted his hands. Mrs Sommetski had been revived and was sobbing in a chair.

We tried to pin him down to the facts. It had been a Number 73 bus, he thought. But the 73 bus going east along Oxford Street went on for about six miles further to Stoke Newington. Normally it was an obvious road; one might chase the bus. But with the bombing, bus routes were completely unpredictable. How could one know which bus it was—if indeed it had been a 73 bus at all. And it was now 4.15.

Everyone was pushing questions at Sommetski, and I heard one of the secretaries ask him whether it could have been a 73-A bus and not a 73. She explained to me that the 73-A didn't go through all the way but turned into a terminus near Islington. There was no way of checking with Sommetski, and with the service so disrupted there was no point in trying to telephone. But the 73-A was the only chance. I ran out of the room and jumped on my motor-bike, roaring down the street with a wild sense of excitement, swooping in and out of the obstructions and aiming as best I knew towards Islington. Once past King's Cross, I had to stop to ask the way, but ultimately I found the terminal and drove in.

The yard was empty. It was quiet and peaceful after the bustle and confusion outside. I hitched my bike on to its stand and ran across to the little office. No one was in a hurry inside the office, and when I finally got hold of the duty clerk, he was quite unruffled at my anxiety. Yes, he told me, the 73-A did come into this terminal. There was one just coming in. I looked through the window and saw the great heart-warming red bus purr slowly through the narrow gate and come throbbingly to rest. The driver got down from his perch in front and stretched himself. The conductor was still on the bus, fiddling with the indicators; then he, too, left it and strolled across to the office, carrying the usual packages of tickets and money.

'Gentleman here asking if anything was left on the bus, Alf,' said the clerk to him.

'Just one thing,' said Alf, producing a little brown bag. My heart began to pound.

'This might be it, eh?' said the clerk to me, opening it and looking inside. 'Can you describe the contents?'

I tried to speak calmly. 'Two passports, name of Sommetski. A big paper with an American stamp on it, same name. And a ship ticket.'

He took the things out and put them on the desk. There they were, the product of years of waiting, centuries of despair. There was a little purse there, too, with two pounds inside. And there were some photographs of a small child.

He put the things back and handed the bag to me. 'Just sign for it,' he said.

'Is there anything to pay?' I managed to ask.

THE SPECIAL CASE

'Oh, yes,' he said. 'We always make a charge, depending on the value. Nothing valuable here, I see. Suppose we say two shillings.'

The bike seemed to sing as I roared back to Holborn House. When I came into the hall, Sommetski and his wife were pacing up and down, whispering together in a restless agony. I held out the bag. Mrs Sommetski went white and fainted away again. Sommetski came towards me tremblingly. It was five o'clock. We gathered them together and rushed them off to Euston.

★ ★ ★

With the last ship gone, I thought I had better find out what was in the official mind about winding up the camp, and I went over the next morning to see Tyrell.

The Office of the Lord Lieutenant, an ancient sinecure, was in a gracious eighteenth-century house off St James's. One wondered what went on there, apart from special operations that were thrust on it, like the internment of enemy aliens. Tyrell, graceful and unregimented, suited the mood of the house perfectly.

He was apparently quite pleased with the way things had gone, and not displeased with my own part. 'You speak German quite well, don't you?' he remarked casually. 'Do you think you could pass as a German?'

A hundred pictures flashed through my mind, including one of a neat little firing party dealing with an agent in civilian clothes. 'Oh, God, no!' I said. 'I'm fluent, but I have a terrible accent.'

'Ah, well,' he murmured. 'We'll think of something else for you. Tell me about Rado Kindler. He's down at Fairbridge. Do you know him?'

My eyes popped a little. 'Oh, yes, I know him,' I said. 'Very good taste in brandy.'

'Yes, so I gather,' said Tyrell. 'Pretty astute, you'd say?'

I agreed that astute was the word.

'We may use him,' Tyrell said. 'Some talk about his going out to South America.'

So many things were being left unsaid that I hesitated to pursue the subject. I wondered if something like a double agent's role was in mind for him. The part suited him, if one could only be sure. But wasn't that the way with double agents? They had to give just this air of being untrustworthy in order to generate the feeling that they could be bought. And suddenly I began to wonder. The lunch. Had this been his way of testing *me*? Rather a sweet thought.

Tyrell had remembered something. 'We've one more ship for you,' he said. 'A Norwegian ship escaped last week and is sailing for New York in two or three days. I've just sent you a message about it. Lots of cabin space. You can have seventy berths.'

★   ★   ★

This time, Stoessel would go. I was determined. I phoned down to Baumgart immediately to tell him about the ship and asked him to make quite sure that Stoessel's papers would be processed in time. I got in touch with the Governor of Wandsworth Gaol to notify him that Mrs Stoessel was to be released for emigration. I sent a message to the American Consul saying that I could personally recommend Stoessel for a visa, that he was an exceptionally pleasant person who deserved a break—that he was, in fact, a special case.

The provision of this unexpected ship with seventy berths seemed like a miracle to the refugees, and everything went with a swing. Messages and paper flashed back and forth, and when the day for departure arrived, and the whole troop was assembled in Holborn House for a final checking of documents, the atmosphere was one of holiday. The Fairbridge contingent had been brought up by bus, wives and children had come in from all over the place, and, greatest joy of all, Mrs Stoessel had been brought up by a warder from Wandsworth and reunited with her husband.

THE SPECIAL CASE

I went with them to Euston. There was an alert on, and occasional bangs. But Stoessel stood outside the station with me to take a last look at London.

'I didn't want to go,' he told me. 'I would have liked to stay. They shouldn't have put my wife in prison. It was a mistake, I know; but I can't stay here now. I wish I could.'

We shook hands and I wandered away. I'd had enough, too. I walked down Southampton Row to Holborn House to pick up my motor-bike, thinking rather sadly, as I caught sight of it waiting for me outside the office, that I should have to give it back now to the Army. The excitement was over. The war stretched ahead, grey and endless.

Perhaps I should have a last talk with Tyrell. I got on the bike and roared the engine a bit driving to St James's. Parking near the Ritz, and realizing that it was lunch-time, I suddenly felt the desire to indulge myself for once. The carpets, the soft lights, the obsequious waiters were balm to the soul. I sat down in the Grill Room, and there across the floor was Kindler, lunching with another man, as elegant as himself, and two beautiful women.

He saw me at the same moment and came across immediately, delighted, it seemed, at the encounter. 'So much pleasanter than Fairbridge,' he said. 'I breathe again.'

'How do you happen to be in London?' I asked him.

'Oh, I got permission to come up and see my dentist,' he said airily. 'They gave me a special guard. There he is, outside.' Sure enough, a Tommy from the camp was sitting waiting in the hall.

'And what have you decided about release?' I asked.

'Well, I'm not quite sure,' he said, cocking his head a little to one side as if weighing the whole thing. 'I think I may be opening an arms factory, making automatic rifles. I'm just discussing it now.' He waved his hand toward his table, where his companions sat drinking champagne.

'Oh, then you've decided to stay in England?'

'No,' he said. 'Not in England. I think I shall be going abroad. More interesting, you know.'

'Abroad? Perhaps South America?'

There was a slight twinkle in his eye. 'Perhaps. Perhaps. There are so many interesting things to do. One has to organize things, don't you think? And now you *must* join us for lunch. I insist. You take things too seriously. You need a change.'

I joined them. He was right. I needed a change.

AND THE CRISPING PINS

KINDLER had said I needed a change, and Providence seemed to agree, judging by what happened. But a change could have been a week in Brighton. Had Providence lost all sense of moderation?

The change I was given was a sudden and utterly unexpected translation to the New World. Tyrell was, it seemed, satisfied with me. There was a very urgent job of a similar kind to be done in the Canadian internment camps, and my experience would be valuable. Preliminary arrangements took about two months, and one day the word came to pack my bags for immediate departure. I packed my bags and took up a seat next to the telephone. About six weeks later I was instructed to join a pathetic little ship that wandered round the icy waters of the North Atlantic all alone for three weeks before it finally managed to reach Halifax.

I had wondered what the children of Israel who left Fairbridge would make of their Promised Land, and now I was to see it myself. As far as I could tell, going down to the United States on my first visit from Canada, New York was as full of strange peoples as the original Canaan. As I walked down Broadway, I seemed to be mingling with all the tribes of Genesis—the Hittites, the Kennizites, the Amorites, the Jebusites. I even thought I could detect a few Girgashites: but of course they may just have been Jebusites with too dark a tan after a long holiday in Miami.

Later, when I got to know New York better, I discovered that there were many other tribes there not even mentioned in the Bible—the Lovestonites, the Townsendites, the Thomasites, the Greenites, and of course the Single Taxers. There were other things there too, not mentioned in the Bible: for one thing, an enormous sense of fun. But for the rest it was mostly a Promised Land as spelt out in the Pentateuch—a land flowing with milk and honey, especially milk. And there was another prediction too. The spies whom Moses sent in to Canaan in the Book of Numbers came back with lots of praise but also with one ominous comment: 'It is a land which devours its inhabitants.' There is just no doubt about it: you can find everything in the Bible.

Everyone knows, of course, that New York is a place of turmoil, while England is full of tranquillity; but looking back now I find myself remembering how tranquil life was, in one sense, in New York, and how disturbed it often is over here. If peace of mind is the test, there is a lot to be said for the whole—and wholesome—acceptance of Jewish existence in New York as against a rather nebulous (or *nebbish*) existence in a land where there are fewer tribes to add a hyphen to one's description. Undoubtedly fifty thousand Park Avenue psycho-analysts (not to mention a thousand Reform Rabbis) will rise up to point out that peace of mind is obtainable anywhere if one goes about it the right way; and perhaps that is where one has to leave this subject. But there is no denying all the same that the Jews of New York have evolved a kind of unconscious philosophy that really takes in everything. One might express it like this: *Gefillte fish is not the whole of life: there is also chopped liver.*

When Kindler said I needed a change and Tyrell obligingly arranged it, I felt sure that what Providence had in mind was something that would shake me out of the preoccupation with Jewish studies that had plagued me for so long. It certainly worked that way to begin with. The Canadian problem that I had to deal with was such a watertight question of administration that it seemed to leave no room for Biblical glosses. To state the problem is easy. The British Government had transferred three thousand enemy alien refugees to Canada for safe-keeping during the invasion threat. Almost all wanted to emigrate to the United States where they had close relatives or friends. The Canadian authorities were perfectly willing to release these internees for emigration if the U.S. authorities would first provide visas for them: the U.S. authorities were perfectly willing to provide visas if the Canadians would first release the refugees from internment. And there the problem stuck—for months.

Neither side would budge. As far as I could remember, this problem had just never arisen in the Bible.

But it was solved through the Bible, as apparently all things can be. And it was marvellous to see that those who solved it had no idea that they were simply acting out a Bible story.

It began for me with a visit to Ruth Draper, the famous diseuse. There was a young Italian boy in one of the Canadian camps whom she was very anxious to get released. His parents, who had fled from Italy to England, were very old friends and she had known the boy from infancy. She had assumed in her innocence that it would be enough to tell the authorities that she was ready to take full responsibility for the boy if he could come to New York, and was baffled to find that red tape prevented it. Moving swiftly into high gear, she had spoken to some personal friends in high places—Mrs Roosevelt, Secretary of State Cordell Hull, Justice Frankfurter, Governor Lehmann and others—but nothing, it seemed, could be done. Now she was not baffled but enraged.

During this time she had been writing to me in Canada urging me to help her protégé, Arturo, and when I was in New York I went to see her. She had always been a marvel to me when I had seen her perform in London, sitting quietly all alone on the stage and filling the theatre with her characters. I discovered that evening how close her art was to her life. In those days everyone who loved England, as she did, was desperate about the London blitz and full of guilt at not sharing it. She wanted to hear about it directly from me; but after supper she took out a letter she had just received from her old London dresser, and began to read it aloud to me and the other two guests. It was a long letter, written with all the natural good humour of a London cockney—a straight description of the odds and ends of life as complicated by the blitz: a funny thing that happened to Bert, Polly's second boy—the one with red hair—knocked off his bike by an explosion on his paper round; old Joe still coming in every night to his corner seat at the pub. She had begun to read the letter quite simply, but within a moment or two she disappeared into the character. From anybody else it might have sounded patronizing. But from her it was infinitely moving to hear that gruff old cockney struggling with the blackout, queuing for cigarettes, clutching her brown paper parcels as she hurried home in the rain to listen to the nine o'clock news. When the letter was finished we sat there, all of us, our cheeks wet with tears. The courage, the humour, the bombs—only in New York could this happen.

We discussed possible strategies for getting Arturo released. I had practically given up hope of a general solution being adopted. Each side was too committed and too obstinate. But if one refugee could somehow be released, it might loosen the whole log-jam.

'Then it isn't selfish of me to press just for Arturo,' Ruth Draper said.

'On the contrary,' I told her. 'If we could get him treated as a special case it might start everything.'

She had a tremendously strong, handsome face. One could hardly imagine anyone resisting that will.

'I'm going up to Ottawa next week,' she said, 'to give a performance in aid of the Canadian Red Cross. I'll go and see some government people while I'm there.'

But what actually happened had been described in the Book of Esther about two thousand years earlier.

She told me the story a week later. 'The Prime Minister, Mackenzie King, came to my performance and gave a big party for me afterwards. He's an old friend and he said to me: "Ruth: you have done so much for Canada: is there anything Canada can do for you?" So I said: "There is a young innocent boy, whom I have known since he was a baby, being held in one of your internment camps behind barbed wire, without offence, without a trial." He turned to one of his aides and said: "Why is this being done?" The man got rather red and said: "Oh, unfortunately there's some regulation . . ." Mackenzie King got very angry and said: "This is outrageous. Release that boy tomorrow into Miss Draper's care and get rid of the regulation."'

Could anything be more literal: King Ahasuerus at the banquet, inviting Esther to name her request: Esther telling the

King of the order issued without his knowledge to destroy the Jews, and the King's reply: *'Who is he and where is he that durst presume in his heart to do this!'*

So there was great rejoicing throughout the land of Persia—or rather Canada. No sooner had Arturo been released, than we applied for ten more boys to be released under guarantee, and within three months all the refugees had been found guarantors of some kind and the problem was solved.

But it really began to look as if I would never get rid of the Bible. And it was even worse when my job in Canada came to an end and I was transferred to a different government job in New York. I stayed there a long time, and the more I saw of it the more Biblical it seemed to me: not the synagogues, of course—those dull abodes of nineteenth-century sanctimony—but everything in New York outside them—the intensity of conviction, the fierceness of intellectual argument, the passion of denunciation, the rigid social separation of the three main tribes—the Protestites, the Catholites and the Jebusites—all against an Old Testament background of pleasure-filled masses ('a people making holiday'), with cynicism and corruption in high places. The prophet Isaiah would have been thoroughly at home.

And the girls! As a schoolboy I had always had a secret yen for all the wicked women denounced by the prophets. They sounded so attractive. And here one had only to walk down Fifth Avenue during the lunch-hour to see them in all their finery, with their beautiful hairdo's and bold eyes. . . .

I told all this to Pat one night as we walked away from the theatre, shortly before I came back to England. It was always fun to try out theories on Pat, especially Jewish theories. She was a quarter Jewish and all-Jewish—like New York itself; and like New York she forced one to push every question further. The truth was lurking somewhere behind all this mess. If it couldn't be pushed out by New York's intensity, where could it?

We were on our way—naturally since Pat was in the theatre herself—to have supper at Sardi's; and there we bumped into her friend Marjorie who was, like Pat, a struggling young actress. They were a wonderful pair to look at across the table—Pat with her big brown eyes and dark hair, and Marjorie, a wild blue-eyed blonde. They had such energy and vitality as they sat there gabbing away at each other, their eyes darting everywhere to see if there was someone at another table whom they should perhaps be saying hallo to.

Pat had been telling Marjorie about our conversation. 'He thinks we're all out of a Cecil B. de Mille production,' she said to her.

'Well, aren't you?' I said. 'The script is all in Isaiah: "*For the daughters of Zion are haughty, and walk with stretched forth necks and wanton eyes, walking and mincing as they go, and making a tinkling with their feet.*" '

'I have never tinkled in my life,' Pat said.

'How do you remember it all?' Marjorie asked me.

'My poor father drummed it all into me,' I said. 'He warned me about you, and I listened too carefully.'

'Is that why you're going back to England?' Pat asked. 'You can't take it?'

'Oh, I can take it,' I said. 'I can take it with me, in fact, thereby disproving an old Red Indian proverb. But of course England will never be the same.'

'But that's just why you shouldn't go back,' Pat said. 'You can't go home again.'

'I don't think I ever left home,' I said.

'I know exactly what you mean,' Marjorie said. 'I feel exactly the same about North Dakota. I'd feel lost if it weren't there somehow in the background.'

'Is that what you mean?' Pat asked me. 'Like that book you told me about—*The Need for Roots*? Doesn't one ever break away? Shouldn't one try?'

'Oh yes, one tries. But it doesn't work too well. You remember Blake:

> '*You throw the sand against the wind*
> *And the wind blows it back again.*'

'There you go again,' Pat said, 'trying to disarm one with a quotation. Just an excuse for not thinking clearly enough. It's true enough that you never left home, but isn't it time that you did? Isn't that just what America is? The place that grew because people left home? Suppose my grandfather—I mean my Jewish one—had stayed on in Pinsk. The world would never have known the bobby pin.' She saw the surprise on my face. 'Have I never told you the story of my grandfather's life? From rags to rags in one generation?'

'He never invented the bobby pin,' Marjorie said disbelievingly.

'My grandfather was a tailor,' Pat said, 'working in a little shop. One day he was repairing an English tweed coat with heavy buttons fixed with a clip at the back—you know the way they are. He got the idea that women could use this as a hair-pin that would stay put and mentioned it to his boss. His boss started manufacturing it and became a millionaire.'

'And that, my dear, is how I met your grandmother,' I said.

'Exactly,' Pat said. 'The boss gave up his shop, my grandfather got a job repairing costumes in a theatre, and there was Grandma—a Swedish nightingale. But there's something lively in the whole process, don't you think?'

'I do, I do. America—the land where everyone's grandfather could have invented the bobby pin. That's all in Isaiah too, only he calls them crisping pins. The trouble is, he says that it's all got to end.'

'I'm sure I don't mind,' Pat said, 'as long as I get to stop that damn tinkling with my feet.'

'Oh, you'll stop more than tinkling,' I said. 'The whole of the New York garment industry has got to come to a standstill. "*In that day the Lord will take away the bravery of their ornaments, the chains, the bracelets and the mufflers, the bonnets, the headbands and the earrings: the suits, the mantles, the wimples and the crisping pins. . . .*" ' I paused for breath. 'And do you know what?' I said to Pat. 'You'll *still* be beautiful.'

It was on this happy loving note that I left America. But I must go back soon on a visit. Where can one enjoy the thought of England as much as in New York?